W9-ABL-898

ATWATER, OHIO 44201

WATERLOO HIGH SCHOOL LIBRARY
1464 INDUSTRY RD.
ATWATER, OHIO 44201

INNER CITY
VIOLENCE

Gary E. McCuen

IDEAS IN CONFLICT SERIES

GARY McCUEN
publications inc.

502 Second Street
Hudson, Wisconsin 54016
Phone (715) 386-7113

303.6
mc

All rights reserved. No part of this book may be reproduced or stored by any means without prior permission from the copyright owner.

Illustration & photo credits

P. Crowley 29, Bill DeOre 144, Ed Gentry 125, Steve Kelley 86, Locher 23, 112, Craig MacIntosh 56, 80, 117, Eleanor Mill 37, 106, Pat Mitchell 93, National Council on Crime and Delinquency 138, David Seavey 18, 51, 62, 68, 91, 99, 149, Stein 131, Richard Wright 44. Cover illustration by Ron Swanson.

publications inc.

©1990 by Gary E. McCuen Publications, Inc.
502 Second Street, Hudson, Wisconsin 54016
(715) 386-7113
International Standard Book Number
0-86596-073-9
Printed in the United States of America

CONTENTS

REASONING SKILL DEVELOPMENT

These activities may be used as individualized study guides for students in libraries and resource centers or as discussion catalysts in small group and classroom discussions.

IDEAS in CONFLICT ®

This series features ideas in conflict on political, social and moral issues. It presents counterpoints, debates, opinions, commentary and analysis for use in libraries and classrooms. Each title in the series uses one or more of the following basic elements:

Introductions that present an issue overview giving historic background and/or a description of the controversy.

Counterpoints and debates carefully chosen from publications, books, and position papers on the political right and left to help librarians and teachers respond to requests that treatment of public issues be fair and balanced.

Symposiums and forums that go beyond debates that can polarize and oversimplify. These present commentary from across the political spectrum that reflect how complex issues attract many shades of opinion.

A global emphasis with foreign perspectives and surveys on various moral questions and political issues that will help readers to place subject matter in a less culture-bound and ethno-centric frame of reference. In an ever shrinking and interdependent world, understanding and cooperation are essential. Many issues are global in nature and can be effectively dealt with only by common efforts and international understanding.

Reasoning skill study guides and discussion activities provide ready made tools for helping with critical reading and evaluation of content. The guides and activities deal with one or more of the following:

RECOGNIZING AUTHOR'S POINT OF VIEW

INTERPRETING EDITORIAL CARTOONS

VALUES IN CONFLICT

WHAT IS EDITORIAL BIAS?

WHAT IS SEX BIAS?
WHAT IS POLITICAL BIAS?
WHAT IS ETHNOCENTRIC BIAS?
WHAT IS RACE BIAS?
WHAT IS RELIGIOUS BIAS?

*From across **the political spectrum** varied sources are presented for research projects and classroom discussions. Diverse opinions in the series come from magazines, newspapers, syndicated columnists, books, political speeches, foreign nations, and position papers by corporations and non-profit institutions.*

About the Editor

Gary E. McCuen is an editor and publisher of anthologies for public libraries and curriculum materials for schools. Over the past 19 years his publications of over 200 titles have specialized in social, moral and political conflict. They include books, pamphlets, cassettes, tabloids, film-strips and simulation games, many of them designed from his curriculums during 11 years of teaching junior and senior high school social studies. At present he is the editor and publisher of the *Ideas in Conflict* series and the *Editorial Forum* series.

CHAPTER 1

LIVING IN FEAR: AN OVERVIEW

LIVING IN FEAR: AN OVERVIEW

DRUGS AND URBAN VIOLENCE

Anthony A. Parker

Anthony A. Parker wrote the following reading in his capacity as the assistant news editor of Sojourners *magazine, an independent Christian monthly.*

Anthony A. Parker, "U.S. Drug Trade Sparks Record Violence," *Sojourners*, March 1989, pp. 10-11. Reprinted with permission from *Sojourners*, Box 29272, Washington, D.C. 20017.

An unprecedented number of murders, linked to the buying and selling of cocaine and other drugs, were recorded in inner cities across the nation in 1988. In New York City and Washington, D.C., in Miami and Houston, the presence of "crack," the street name for a derivative of cocaine, has altered the lives of thousands. Few areas around the country were spared the violence that has become associated with crack. The statistics are staggering.

Violence and Crack

Washington, D.C., had the highest number of murders per capita in the nation, with 60 murders per 100,000 people. Detroit followed close behind with 50 murders per 100,000; Atlanta's rate was 51; New Orleans was fourth with 43; and Dallas had 36 murders per 100,000 people.

Several cities across the nation reported big increases in the total number of murders committed in 1988 over 1987. Washington, D.C., recorded 372 murders in 1988 and had the largest increase, one of 65 percent; Houston's murder rate increased 38 percent to 465 murders; Miami's murder rate increased 29 percent to 296 murders; Philadelphia had an increase of 19 percent with 402 murders; and New York City went up by 12 percent with 1,867 murders. Police in each city say that crack is the main reason for the dramatic increases in murders.

Crack is "the worst drug ever," a homicide detective in Miami said. "There is no such thing as a recreational crack cocaine user. They are all terribly addicted. Young people are willing to kill for it," the detective said.

Crack is essentially a poor person's drug. For as little as $5, a "rock" of crack sends a user on a very brief but very intense high. The medical community says that once a person uses crack, he or she is hooked. But a common side effect of crack use is violent, volatile mood swings.

Washington, D.C., is an unfortunate example of what crack is doing across the country. Sixty-one percent of the murders committed in the nation's capital in 1988 were drug-related. Guns were used to inflict 72 percent of the murders. More than 80 percent of the victims were black, and their average age was 29.

Isaac Fulwood Jr., the District's assistant chief of police for field operations, told *Sojourners* that 1988 was a turning point. "When you look at the 372 murders in the District of Columbia, with 82 percent of them being black males, and you look at the

┌───┐
│
A HUMAN SHIELD

While walking home with his mother and two-year-old brother at mid-day, three-year-old Greg Alvarez was caught in a cross-fire between rival drug gangs. As Greg's mother crouched behind a parked car to protect her children, Greg was snatched from her grasp by one of the combatants—himself only 18 years old—and was used as a human shield. With Greg held up in front of the snatcher, his rivals callously disregarded the safety of this child, and fired away at their target. While Greg was frantically screaming "Mommy, Mommy," a bullet pierced his left arm, passed through his chest, and exited on the right side. Fortunately, he lived.

Excerpted from remarks of Honorable Edward Koch, mayor of New York City, before the United States Conference on Mayors, February 7, 1989
│
└───┘

impact on the quality of life, you can never go back to business as usual or being the same person."

Battles for Turf

Every day Fulwood encounters the death and destruction caused by crack. "If you've seen people dying on the streets, being shot, their bodies being literally shattered, and if you happen to live in one of these neighborhoods where they have open-air drug markets that precipitate all this violence, then you quickly realize that there is something wrong in our society where people feel that they can kill another human being."

It has not always been this way, according to Fulwood. "In the '70s there was a heroin epidemic. But you did not see the violence we are seeing now. In the '80s we started to see PCP and its violence. Over the last two or three years, it started to be crack and the amount of violence associated with it."

One of the reasons for the violence associated with crack, according to Fulwood, is that the market is unorganized. There is no one dominant gang that controls the sale of cocaine in the inner city. As a result, many of those killed were involved in battles for turf.

There are, however, tragic exceptions. In Washington, D.C., a woman was killed by a stray bullet that crashed through her kitchen window during a gun battle outside her home. Another

11

teen-age woman was killed outside a nightclub by drug dealers shooting randomly from a passing car. In Boston, a 12-year-old girl was killed on her doorstep by drug dealers looking for a neighbor's son. In Los Angeles, "drive-by" shootings in the war between the rival gangs have terrorized innocent bystanders for months and claimed scores of lives.

Drug Entrepreneurs

The emotional impact on the families and friends of those killed by drug violence cannot be measured, according to Fulwood. "It's not just the victim dying. This person that died belonged to somebody. They are somebody's parent, son, daughter, and friend. They leave behind the anguish of trying to adjust to the fact that this person is no longer going to be there."

The fluidity of crack trafficking provides an opportunity for many young free-lancers to establish themselves as drug entrepreneurs. They depend on violence to stay in business.

An example of this in Washington, D.C., according to Fulwood, is the fact that there were 1,200 drug-related shootings last year. The reasons for the shootings are varied: drug dealers protecting their turf, fending off rival dealers, or simply using violence to instill fear. "We know of cases where an enforcer for a drug group will come into an area and kill a person in front of a whole lot of people for the sole purpose of controlling people and making a point," Fulwood said. "If you don't conform, then you're killed."

The increase in the number of drug-related deaths and shootings is no less disturbing than the viciousness with which they are committed. "It's not enough to kill," said Bernard Cohen, a sociologist at the City University of New York. "You degrade the body. He's dead already with two bullets, so you shoot him with six. You decapitate him, or something else."

Fulwood said many police officers report seeing wounds reminiscent of injuries they saw while fighting in Vietnam. Some of the 1,200 shootings reported in Washington involved men who had their kneecaps or testicles shot off.

High-Tech Weapons

Such wounds can only be made by high-powered weapons, which are becoming standard features in the drug trade. Such weapons have given drug dealers a clear advantage over the police. Uzi machine guns, AK-47 assault rifles, crossbows, automatic handguns, silencers, and bulletproof vests have replaced the type of weapons formerly associated with drugs.

12

Many police departments around the country are replacing their old .38 revolvers with 9 millimeter semi-automatic pistols.

Drug dealers who own high-tech weapons, while having already proven that they will use them against each other, have begun to demonstrate that they are willing to turn them on police officers. Last February, a rookie New York City police officer was murdered in broad daylight while guarding the home of a drug witness.

Values and Choices

The fear that is caused by violence is hard to break through, according to Fulwood. "It's very difficult to deal with the element of fear in terms of mobilizing the community. When you talk to people they say, 'It's just me by myself. If I go to court, the police department can't protect me. I'm at the mercy of the drug dealer because I saw him kill someone.'"

Fulwood believes one person can make a difference. It involves values and choices people make concerning their lives, he says. This is particularly important where children and young people are concerned. Selling crack is a quick way to get the "finer things in life" that kids in the inner city would not otherwise have. This is, perhaps, the greatest tragedy for Fulwood: young people "making choices based purely on dollars and cents."

The allure of becoming rich means that many young people "won't take a job at McDonald's or some job that pays less than a lot of money." Fulwood recalls a conversation he had with a young man: "Why should I go and make $3.25 or $4.50 an hour at a regular job? I can make that in one minute on the street. And I can make $400 an hour if I want to. . . .How much do you make, Chief?"

When Fulwood told the man his police department salary, he laughed at Fulwood, and said, "You think you're doing good, but I can make more than that."

Missing Hope

Such an attitude is not deterred by the thought of going to jail. "Many drug dealers run their operation from jail," according to Fulwood. The threat of jail, death, or permanent injury is considered a "business risk." Fulwood knows of several occasions when young men being booked for murder have had "smirks" on their faces, and have told the arresting officers "to do what you have to do." Attitudes like that reflect a lack of values, according to Fulwood, and cannot be changed simply by making more arrests.

For this reason, Fulwood believes that celebrated anti-drug programs, such as the District's Operation Cleansweep, are not enough. The Washington program cost $6 million over 28 months, and resulted in 45,000 arrests. Yet Washington still had the highest murder rate in the country. Other cities plan to invest millions of dollars in special narcotics units to combat drugs. While some programs have been successful in reducing drug violence, most cities report that the dealers simply move to a new location.

What is missing in these people's lives, says Fulwood, is hope. "There are so many young black men who have their entire lives ahead of them. But he's got to have a 4x4 truck, a big car, expensive jewelry, designer clothes. . . .He's got what he wants right now, and doesn't care about the impact of his behavior on other people."

LIVING IN FEAR: AN OVERVIEW

VIOLENCE AGAINST WOMEN

Holly Littlefield

Holly Littlefield wrote this article in her capacity as a high school
English teacher. Her story originally appeared in the Minneapolis
Star-Tribune.

Holly Littlefield, "At Home and in the Street, Living a Life Punctuated by Fear,"
Minneapolis Star Tribune, October 28, 1988. Reprinted by permission of the *Star*
Tribune, Newspaper of the Twin Cities.

I am afraid. It's been a gradual realization, but slowly it has dawned on me that although I live in one of the world's richest and most advanced countries—in one of its safest and most progressive cities—I am nearly always afraid. I don't walk around with a gun in my hand, my eyes darting furtively at every corner, body tensed, wondering what will jump out at me. But always in the back of my mind is the thought: Be careful—someone might hurt you.

Fear and Anger

I did laundry last night. Nothing particularly strange or unique about that. I gathered together my laundry basket, keys, soap, quarters and left my apartment—heading for the basement of my building. I was thinking more about the book I was reading than about the laundry I had to do. When I opened the laundry-room door, however, all thoughts of books and laundry left my mind. I felt my body stiffen and my heart race. Along with the washer and dryer stood a man.

He wasn't holding a knife; he didn't even look suspicious. He was simply sorting his socks and singing along with his headset. I stood in the doorway a moment unsure of what to do, then turned and went back to my apartment. I found the prospect of a few minutes alone in the basement laundry room with a strange man too disconcerting—that voice in my head muttering, "be careful, be careful."

So, yes, I am afraid. I have three locks on my door; I carry mace. My car doors are always locked. I never park in ramps and I don't go downtown anymore. That voice in my head won't let me.

Sometimes at night I lie alone and listen to the creaks and shifts in my apartment that I'm sure I've never heard before, and even though all the curtains are closed, I get the strangest feeling that someone is watching me. I know I'm being silly, but I'm still afraid.

But even more than that, I am angry. I listened to the stories about Carrie Coonrod and Mary Foley* and I thank God that I cannot even begin to imagine what their deaths must have been

---

*Editor's note: Carrie Coonrod and Mary Foley were murdered, in separate incidents, in downtown Minneapolis parking ramps during 1988.

TAKE BACK THE STREETS

Law-abiding citizens, already fearful, see things occurring that make them even more fearful. A vicious cycle begins of fear-induced behavior increasing the sources of that fear.

A Los Angeles police sergeant put it this way: "When people in this district see that a gang has spray-painted its initials on all the stop signs, they decide that the gang, not the people or the police, controls the streets. When they discover that the Department of Transportation needs three months to replace the stop signs, they decide that the city isn't as powerful as the gang. These people want us to help them take back the streets." Painting gang symbols on a stop sign or a storefront is not, by itself, a serious crime. As an incident, it is trivial. But as the symptom of a problem, it is very serious.

James Q. Wilson and George L. Kelling, "Making Neighborhoods Safe," The Atlantic Monthly, *February 1989*

like. It's made me furious with a system that seems to value the criminal more than his victims. After at least 17 rapes, a man was released to rape and kill again? Will they let him out again in another few years? In California, a man is released only eight years after brutally raping a young girl and then cutting off her arms. The list of examples seems endless. Now we hear that the prison term for rape averages about two years—without treatment.

A Violent Society

It's clear that our society is becoming more and more violent. Our courts condone it. Give a kid three years for ax murdering four people; release a man to rape and rape and rape and finally kill. Why does the criminal-justice system bend over backwards to protect the precious rights of those who take the most basic right—to live without fear—away from the rest of us? I am tired of a system that serves criminals with plea bargains, light sentences, technicalities and paroles but ignores the victims and the society that it is meant to protect. When will we declare that it is not acceptable to rape and maim and terrorize and kill? When will we make completely certain that no one ever does it twice? When will we stop the second, third and 17th chances? When can we feel safe again? One senator recently pointed out

Boys' night out

Cartoon by David Seavey. Copyright 1989, *USA Today*. Reprinted with permission.

that long prison terms and the death penalty don't deter crime. Perhaps they don't, but they definitely keep those criminals from hurting more people.

The night breeze blows against my curtains. The trees rustle. The moon is full; the stars are out and I look longingly from my window into the cool, calm, inviting night. I want to walk in the peacefulness of the evening with the wind blowing through my hair and the tensions emptying from my mind. But I cannot. I remember Carrie Coonrod and Mary Foley and all the others and that voice in my mind says no. Instead I recheck the locks on my door and go to bed—afraid.

LIVING IN FEAR: AN OVERVIEW

ANTI-GAY VIOLENCE

National Gay and Lesbian Task Force

In this reading, the National Gay and Lesbian Task Force describes anti-gay violence, a rapidly growing concern in our society.

Excerpted from the testimony of the National Gay and Lesbian Task Force before the House Subcommittee on Criminal Justice of the House Committee on the Judiciary, October 9, 1986.

The National Gay and Lesbian Task Force (NGLTF) is America's oldest and largest national gay civil rights organization. We thank you for holding this historic hearing today to examine an alarming and much-overlooked problem facing gay and lesbian Americans.

As you know, the gay community is battling AIDS, one of the deadliest epidemics in recent history. But we are also battling a second epidemic, one that has received far less attention by our public officials. That epidemic is anti-gay violence.

What Is Anti-Gay Violence?

It, too, can be deadly. For many who survive, it leaves physical and emotional scars that will never fade. It has been around long before AIDS, but there is disturbing evidence that the AIDS and anti-gay violence epidemics may now be following the same menacing curve. For, inasmuch as AIDS has spread, so has the fear and hatred that spawns violence. Sadly, our government's answer to anti-gay violence is similar to its initial response to the AIDS epidemic: It is viewed as just a gay problem and therefore not of concern to all society.

What is anti-gay violence? What are its causes? We define it as any violence directed against persons because they are gay or lesbian or perceived to be so. It is motivated by hatred and by the perception that gay people are "easy targets."

Staggering Statistics

Given widespread ignorance about the magnitude of the problem, the National Gay and Lesbian Task Force undertook a study involving nearly 2,100 respondents nationwide.[1] The results were staggering: More than 1 in 5 gay men and nearly 1 in 10 lesbians had been physically assaulted because of their sexual orientation.

More than 40 percent had been threatened with violence. Overall, more than 90 percent had experienced some type of victimization. All this simply for being gay or lesbian. We found that anti-gay violence occurred not only on the street, but also in our schools and even in our homes.

Despite its limitations, our study has been widely praised by sociologists and criminologists. Our findings have been confirmed by local and state studies, which have shown similar high rates of harassment and violence.

One study[2] in Philadelphia concluded that gay people in that city were four times more likely to be victims of violent crimes

VIOLENCE AGAINST GAYS

Seventy gays were killed last year as part of an "alarmingly widespread" pattern of violence and harassment against gay people, the National Gay and Lesbian Task Force said in a report . . . .

While most of the crimes were committed by individuals, the report noted a "disturbing trend" of violence by hate groups, led by neo-Nazi "skinheads." Nineteen organizations in 17 communities reported threats or attacks against gays by such groups last year, the report said.

"*Violence Against Gays Reported to Be 'Alarmingly Widespread,'*" Star Tribune, *June 8, 1989, p. 17A*

than persons in the general urban population.

Anti-Gay Violence Victims

The toll of anti-gay violence cannot be measured solely in terms of these statistics. These numbers do not measure the anguish, fear and loss experienced by Dee, who is still recovering from burns caused by acid thrown at her face when she was leaving the Los Angeles Gay Community Center.

Or by Robert from New Jersey, where assailants beat him, extinguished cigarettes in his face, and then tied him to the back of a truck, dragging him in tow.

Or by the family and friends of Charlie Howard of Maine, who was thrown off a bridge to his death by three teenagers. Or by the members of a Gay Christian congregation in Jacksonville, Florida, whose church was twice set on fire in just one year. Attacks against that church became so frequent that bullet-proof windows had to be installed.

The nightmare for anti-gay violence victims does not end when their assailants have finished with them. Those few who are brave enough to step forward are often revictimized by the very agencies responsible for protecting and helping them. All too often, the police and criminal justice system blame gay victims and fail to vigorously investigate, prosecute, and punish anti-gay crimes.

An Ignored Issue

A few law enforcement agencies represented here today have

Cartoon by Locher. Reprinted by permission: Tribune Media Services..

taken positive steps to remedy this situation, but they are the exception rather than the norm.

This administration has taken a strong stand against international terrorism, both in word and deed. Why is it that so little is said, let alone done, about terrorism within our borders, terrorism against not only the gay community, but also people of color, Jews, recent immigrants, and abortion clinics?

In recent years, the National Gay and Lesbian Task Force has appealed to a variety of federal agencies, and yet little has been done to study or remedy this problem. Indeed, one Justice Department office has actually sought to curb efforts by its grant recipients to address the needs of gay crime victims.

With a few exceptions, the local and state response is hardly more encouraging. A few local programs that assist gay and lesbian victims have received public support. But in most communities, this issue is ignored.

While the official response to anti-gay violence has been disappointing thus far, we still believe that our government has the capacity to respond in a compassionate and effective way to this problem.

---

1 Anti-gay Victimization, a study by the National Gay Task Force (June 1984).

2 Anti-gay Victimization, a report by the Philadelphia Lesbian and Gay Task Force (1985).

WATERLOO HIGH SCHOOL LIBRARY
1464 INDUSTRY RD.
ATWATER, OHIO 44201

LIVING IN FEAR: AN OVERVIEW

VIOLENCE AGAINST THE ELDERLY

Blanche Zidonik

Blanche Zidonik—a 70-year-old grandmother at the time of her testimony—told a congressional subcommittee about violence against the elderly. Specifically, Ms. Zidonik describes an attack that she suffered at the front door of her own home.

Excerpted from the testimony of Blanche Zidonik before the House Select Committee on Aging, October 22, 1985.

I appreciate the opportunity to come to Washington to tell my story to this committee. I hope that it will do some good and serve as both a lesson and a warning to people. . . .

Attack at the Front Door

On October 24, 1984, between the time of 10:30 and 11:00 p.m. I was mugged at my front door. I had just returned home from my son's home where I had been babysitting.

I am a very cautious person and when I am alone, especially after dark, I check the rear view mirror of my car when I turn into the street to be sure that no one is following me. When I pull into the driveway—I didn't have a garage at this time—I park the car and get my key ready to get into the house, and check the general area to be sure no one is lurking around, and then proceed to go in. The street is well-lit, particularly at that point. My house is well-lit. I have spotlights in back. The front door light is on at night, and lights in my house are arranged by timers. I even leave radios on to try to create the impression that someone is home. I have deadbolt locks on all my doors including the basement door and my bedroom door, every door, I guess, except the refrigerator door.

As I was putting my key in the door I heard dry leaves crunch on my front lawn, and turned slightly, expecting to see a neighbor. I quickly realized it was a stranger. He started running toward me. I guess he planned to creep up on me, really, and because I was in an awkward position, it was difficult for me to turn fast. He was apparently not bothered by the fact that the lights were bright and I could see his face very clearly. At that moment I was more startled than I was frightened.

As I turned he pulled his arm back and proceeded to sock me on the jaw. My pocketbook strap was wrapped around my arm. I would gladly have given him my pocketbook, but he pulled at it. In doing so he pulled me down on my right leg and created an injury that is probably permanent. At that point he started running away and I started screaming, "Help, police. Please call the police." Later I learned that the switchboard lit up at the police headquarters as I watched him run down the street.

Now, I am an amateur portrait artist and I just naturally observe people's coloring, features, and so on, so I remember him very, very well. I will never, ever, forget him.

When I watched him go down the street, I waited until he turned and then I attempted to get in the house. I managed to get up, get in the house, and call the police, who said they were on their way because somebody had called. I then called my

VIOLENT CRIME

Crime. Violent crime. It's everywhere. We are all at risk. One in 133 of us will be murdered, the Justice Department estimates. Five of six will be robbed, raped, assaulted.

No wonder people, even in small towns, are putting bars on their windows. No wonder even rural residents lock their gates behind them. They're scared.

That's no way to live. Families are being held prisoners in their own homes. Criminals are controlling the streets.

"President Is Right to Focus on Crime," USA Today, May 16, 1989

son who came down shortly thereafter. I went with my son and the officers who answered the call to police headquarters and I gave a description of what happened, and a complete description of the mugger. A few days later a state police artist did a sketch from my description. To my knowledge he has not been apprehended yet.

The Aftereffects of the Attack

It is just two days short of one year since this has happened and I have been very much affected by the experience. I no longer feel comfortable living alone, yet there is very little I can do about that. Because I was unable to do many things by myself after the injury and depended more on my daughter, I was forced to sell my home in Springfield; I had lived there 38 years. Believe me, I miss my friends and neighbors and activities there, and I have moved to a condominium in Manalapan. This move was not easy.

My right leg was injured so badly I was no longer able to drive. I had to go to the J. F. Kennedy Rehabilitation Center and take lessons to drive with my left foot. That cost about $45 an hour and I spent over $200 to learn to drive again. I had to spend another $100 to have my car fixed so that I could drive with my left foot.

For about six months I was under the care of six doctors, then two doctors, and now one doctor. I have been x-rayed and had CAT scans. I have been examined and treated with electromyography on two different occasions, and it was necessary until this March to have daily therapy with exercises and a quadraflex neuromuscular stimulator. This stimulator cost me $129 a month to rent. I had to do this at home because I was then unable to drive, and my daughter couldn't take me because her house is about a 40-minute drive from Springfield.

All of this has been very painful, very frustrating, and very expensive. It has been difficult for my family as well. Although I can now drive again, I still cannot work, and have been forced to do without the income I made doing secretarial work before my injury. I am still under the doctor's care.

Fortunately, though, I have been reimbursed nearly $1,100 by the New Jersey Violent Crimes Compensation Board for a portion of my medical bills which Medicare and insurance did not pay. I also received a small disability payment for 25 weeks through the disability program of the New Jersey Department of Labor. I am extremely grateful for these sources of assistance, but I have still been forced to reach into my own savings for other medical bills and related expenses.

I hope that some day I will be able to return to work at least part time. But no matter how capable you are—and I am capable—it is not easy for a 70-year-old to find a job.

Senior Citizens Are Vulnerable

The quality of life should be wonderful at this point but it is not. Many people have suffered these dastardly crimes. People of all ages have been assaulted. It is particularly hard on senior citizens. They are especially vulnerable because they cannot react as quickly. They can be more seriously injured because of their age, and as a result, they just depend on others when independence is so important to their happiness and their reason for living.

When older individuals can maintain reasonably good physical ability, they can be helpful, not only to themselves but to others, and make life worthwhile. That is what we are all living for, to feel life is worthwhile. When you get old, you get to realize you are getting close to the time for death. You begin to feel very unnecessary in the usual stream of things. When something like this happens it really enhances all those feelings. It is a very depressing thing, very hard to cope with.

I am really not here to wring my hands and decry my fate. I am 70 years old and I have learned at least that in 70 years, that when things happen to you, you have to take it, pick yourself up, and carry on. But that doesn't mean that these crooks should get away with it. They shouldn't. . . .

I find myself a much more nervous person. I went to put the

28

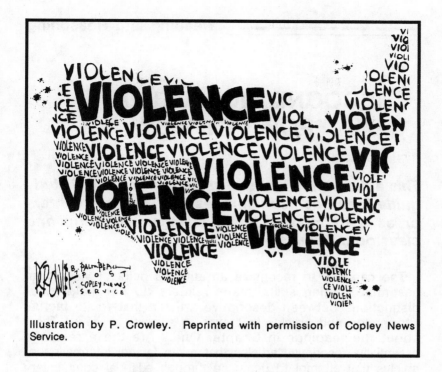

Illustration by P. Crowley. Reprinted with permission of Copley News Service.

garbage out the other night and suddenly I realized it was dark out, and I became very frightened. I felt like somebody was watching me and I quickly got into the house. I am not used to feeling this way. I am used to being independent, and unafraid of things generally. . . .

Too many people don't want to fight back. The fear I see on my friends' faces is outrage and shock, and it is shocking to see. We must overcome this fear, and the way to do it is to fight back and obtain justice for the victim as well as the criminal.

RECOGNIZING AUTHOR'S POINT OF VIEW

This activity may be used as an individualized study guide for students in libraries and resource centers or as a discussion catalyst in small group and classroom discussions.

The capacity to recognize an author's point of view is an essential reading skill. Many readers do not make clear distinctions between descriptive articles that relate factual information and articles that express a point of view. Think about the readings in Chapter One. Are these readings essentially descriptive articles that relate factual information or articles that attempt to persuade through editorial commentary and analysis?

Guidelines

1. Read through the following source descriptions. Choose one of the source descriptions that best describes each reading in Chapter One.

Source Descriptions

a. **Essentially an article that relates factual information**
b. **Essentially an article that expresses editorial points of view**
c. **Both of the above**
d. **None of the above**

2. After careful consideration, pick out one source that you agree with the most. Be prepared to explain the reasons for your choice in a general class discussion.

3. Choose one of the source descriptions above that best describes the other readings in this book.

CHAPTER 2

THE RISE IN URBAN VIOLENCE

THE RISE IN URBAN VIOLENCE

THE CENTRAL CITY: IN SEARCH OF ECONOMIC AND SOCIAL JUSTICE

1988 Commission on the Cities

On the eve of the twentieth anniversary of the Kerner Report, to assess the present situation, a citizen-organized 1988 Commission on the Cities sponsored a national conference on "The Kerner Report: Twenty Years Later." The conference was co-sponsored by the Institute for Public Policy of the University of New Mexico and the Johnson Foundation.

Points to Consider:

1. Compare the number of poor Americans in 1986 with the number of poor Americans in 1969.

2. How have the poverty rates changed in America's central cities? In what ways has urban poverty become deeper and more persistent?

3. Is America becoming two separate societies? Provide examples to support your answer.

4. Describe the "quiet riots" that are taking place in America's major cities. How are these "quiet riots" more destructive than the violent riots of the 1960s?

1988 Commission on the Cities, National Conference: "The Kerner Report Twenty Years Later." This reading was excerpted from *The Kerner Report Updated: Report of the 1988 Commission on the Cities,* March 1, 1988.

The Kerner Report warning is coming true: America is again becoming two separate societies, one black (and, today, we can add Hispanic), one white— separate and unequal.

For a time following the Kerner Report*, America made progress on all fronts—from the late 1960s through the mid-1970s. Then came a series of severe economic shocks that hit the most vulnerable hardest. Poverty is worse now for black Americans, Hispanic Americans, American Indians, and other minorities. But not just for them. The rise in unemployment and poverty has cut across racial and ethnic lines—and affects both blacks and other minorities and whites. (More whites than minority people are poor.). . .

Poverty increased. Census figures show that in 1986, 32.4 million Americans were poor (compared with 24.1 million in 1969). This included about 22 million whites, nearly 9 million blacks, and about 5 million Hispanics. . . .

Cuts in Social Programs

Efforts to cut education, housing, job training, and other social programs became more determined. These efforts were largely successful.

Today, less than one percent of the federal budget is spent for education, down from two percent in 1980. Job training and job subsidization programs were cut nearly 70 percent—from $9 billion in 1981 to only $4 billion.

Less than one percent of the federal budget is now spent on training and job programs. Yet, that part of the federal budget spent on the military has increased from 35 percent in 1980 to 41 percent today. . . .

---

*Editor's note: On July 28, 1967, President Lyndon Johnson appointed the Kerner Commission to study the racial disorders that had occurred in many of America's major cities. The Kerner Report—issued March 1, 1968—called for great new efforts to combat American poverty, unemployment, racism, and the problems of the cities.

```
┌─────────────────────────────────────────────────────┐
│                                                     │
```

WHITE AMERICANS AND THE GHETTO

Segregation and poverty have created in the racial ghetto a destructive environment totally unknown to most white Americans.

What white Americans have never fully understood—but what the Negro can never forget—is that white society is deeply implicated in the ghetto. White institutions created it, white institutions maintain it, and white society condones it.

It is time now to turn with all the purpose at our command to the major unfinished business of this nation. It is time to adopt strategies for action that will produce quick and visible progress. It is time to make good the promises of American democracy to all citizens—urban and rural, white and black, Spanish-surname, American Indian, and every minority group.

Report of the President's National Advisory Commission on Civil Disorders (The Kerner Commission), *1968*

Poverty Worsened and Deepened

The gap between the rich and poor widened. In 1986, the top one-fifth of American households received 46.1 percent of total income, up from 43.3 percent in 1970, while the income share of the middle three-fifths declined from 52.7 percent to 50.2 percent and that of the poorest one-fifth of households went down from 4.1 percent to 3.8 percent.

Census figures also show that poverty has become more prevalent in America's central cities. There, the poverty rates rose by half from 1969 to 1985—increasing from 12.7 percent to 19 percent, a much steeper rise than for those outside.

Poverty has deepened. Typical poor people of the 1980s living in big cities are farther below the poverty line than their unfortunate counterparts of the 1960s. There was a sharp increase between 1970 and 1982 in the percentage of poor people with incomes less than 75 percent of the poverty line.

Urban poverty has become more persistent. According to Professor Greg J. Duncan of the University of Michigan's Survey Research Center, "the chances a poor person in a highly urbanized county would escape his poverty have fallen substantially since the 1970s," after some improvement between the late 1960s and mid-1970s, and are now well below the levels of twenty years ago. . . .

Lack of Vigorous Affirmative Action

Though the Supreme Court has several times recently upheld affirmative action in hiring and promotions, the Reagan Administration has been hostile to affirmative action efforts and to the vigorous enforcement of civil rights laws. . . .

Cutbacks in affirmative action enforcement have been unfortunate, especially because earlier such efforts had been successful in increasing jobs and influence for blacks and in recruiting more blacks into higher education. Affirmative action worked. . . .

More "Separate Societies"

The Kerner Report warning is coming true: America *is* again becoming two separate societies, one black (and, today, we can add Hispanic), one white—separate and unequal.

While there are few all-white neighborhoods, and there is some integration even in black neighborhoods, segregation by race still sharply divides America's cities—in both housing and schools for blacks, and especially in schools for Hispanics. This despite increases in suburbanization and the numbers of blacks and other minorities who have entered the middle class.

For the big cities studied by the Kerner Commission, housing segregation has changed little, if any, and is worse in terms of housing costs for blacks, who are more likely than whites to be renters. Segregation is not just a matter of income; it still cuts across income and education levels. Studies show continued discrimination in housing sales and rentals and in mortgage financing for blacks and Hispanics.

Segregation breeds further inequality for blacks and other minorities—including lessened opportunities for work and the greater likelihood of inferior education.

Segregated housing produces segregated schools, and these are most often worse schools than those available to the children of whites.

From 1968 to 1984, the number of white students in the public schools dropped by 19 percent, while the number of black students increased by 2 percent. Hispanic student numbers skyrocketed, up 80 percent.

Public schools are becoming more segregated. There has been no national school desegregation progress since the last favorable Supreme Court decision in this field in 1972. . . .

Illustration by Eleanor Mill.

Greater Racial Contrast

Non-white unemployment in 1968 was 6.7 percent, compared to 3.2 percent for whites. Today, black unemployment is more than double white unemployment.

Median black family income, as a percentage of median white family income, dropped from 60 percent in 1968 to 57.1 percent in 1986. Those who would be classified as "working poor," if they were white—those with annual incomes between $9,941 and $18,700—are the middle class for black families; that is the present range of median black family income.

From these facts of black and Hispanic segregation and inequality, Professor Orfield has concluded that the ghettos and barrios of America's cities are "separate and deteriorating societies, with separate economies, increasingly divergent family structures and basic institutions, and even growing linguistic separation. The physical separation by race, class, and economic situation is much greater than it was in the 1960s, the level of impoverishment, joblessness, educational inequality, and housing even more severe."

The Urban Underclass

The result is a persistent, large, and growing American urban underclass.

Poverty is both urban and rural, both white and minority. But the great majority of the nation's poor people—70.4 percent in 1985—live in metropolitan areas. From 1974 to 1983, over 33 percent of highly-urban population (those living in the nation's 56 most highly-urban counties) were poor at least once, and 5.2 percent were poor at least 80 percent of the time. During the same period, 60 percent of blacks in these areas were poor at least once, and 21.1 percent were poor at least 80 percent of the time.

Central-city poverty has become more concentrated. From 1974 to 1985, in central-city poverty tracts with a poverty rate of 20 percent or more, the numbers of people living in poverty nearly doubled—from 4.1 million to 7.8 million. In areas of extreme poverty—more than 40 percent—the numbers of white families living in poverty went up 44 percent, the numbers of black families 104 percent, and the numbers of Hispanic families 300 percent.

University of Chicago sociologist William Julius Wilson has found a resulting "rapid social deterioration" in the inner-city neighborhoods since the Kerner Report, with "sharp increases in social dislocation and the massive breakdown of social institutions in ghetto areas."

Concentrated poverty is "one of the legacies of racial and class oppression," Professor Wilson has stated, and it has produced what he has termed "concentration effects"—the "added constraints and severe restrictions of opportunities associated with living in a neighborhood in which the population is overwhelmingly socially disadvantaged—constraints and opportunities with regard to access to jobs, good schools and other public services, and availability of marriageable partners." The result in these concentrated, central-city areas, he has said, is "sharp increases in joblessness, poverty, and the related problems of single-parent households, welfare dependency, housing deterioration, educational failure, and crime."

National Security Requires New Human Investment

"Quiet riots" are taking place in America's major cities: unemployment, poverty, social disorganization, segregation, family disintegration, housing and school deterioration, and crime.

These "quiet riots" may not be as alarming or as noticeable to outsiders—unless they are among the high proportion of Americans who are victimized by crime—but they are even more destructive of human life than the violent riots of twenty years ago.

This destruction of our human capital is a serious threat to America's national security. The Kerner Report said: "It is time to make good the promises of American democracy to all citizens—urban and rural, white and black, Spanish-surname, American Indian, and every minority group."

Such a recommitment now to that kind of human investment could begin to move us once again toward becoming a more stable and secure society of self-esteem.

6 THE RISE IN URBAN VIOLENCE

THE CENTRAL CITY: IN SEARCH OF CRIMINAL JUSTICE

Allan C. Brownfeld

Allan C. Brownfeld wrote the following reading for Human Events, *a national conservative weekly.*

Points to Consider:

1. Describe the problems associated with bail, parole, furlough, and probation programs.

2. Define the term "career criminal."

3. What is the correlation between the decline in our criminal justice system and the increase in crime itself?

4. How does the author explain American society's refusal to punish serious criminals?

Allan C. Brownfeld, "How Our Criminal Justice System Serves Convicts," *Human Events,* April 22, 1989, pp. 12-15.

Rather than wringing our hands about the escalating rate of violence in our cities, let us finally act to put it to an end.

Murder and other crimes of violence are proliferating in an unprecedented manner in American cities, fueled largely by narcotics. In New York City, 1988 was a record-breaking year—with 1,840 homicides. "People do not feel safe in the streets, nor do they feel safe in their homes," said Sheldon Pulaski, a community leader in Brooklyn. "That's why we have so many burglar alarms, so many houses with bars on the windows." . . .

Washington Post columnist William Raspberry writes that "The civil authorities have lost control of the city's streets. It's time to bring out the troops. Somebody has got to stop the killing." Frances Cress Welsing, a Washington psychiatrist noted for her work with adolescents, says that the city's warring drug dealers "are like children out of behavior control; there's nobody with the authority to say: 'This must stop.' You have to use force to stop the violence." . . .

Criminals on Probation

Many of the most celebrated murder cases in the recent past involve killers who were once in the hands of the law, once in prison, but were released and put back into the streets, only to take the lives of additional innocent victims. . . .

In New York City, more than half of all criminals on probation commit crimes while they are under court ordered supervision, according to a study released in January 1989 by Comptroller Harrison Goldin. "Probation in New York is a disaster," Goldin said. "It is a flop to sentence career criminals to probation. It simply is a license that allows them out to continue their criminal career."

In Goldin's report, of the 58 criminals arrested while on probation, seven had been arrested five or more times. One had been arrested 12 times. The report recommended that probation be denied to ex-convicts and that a state law be passed forbidding judges to give probation to repeat offenders. . . .

The same criminals are victimizing innocent citizens over and over again—because our legal system returns them to the community. More than four-fifths of our prisoners are recidivists, with nearly 60 percent of them having been incarcerated at least

---

DRUGS AND VIOLENT CRIME

From Los Angeles to Washington, drugs and violent crime are making our cities unlivable. Problems that were once only associated with the "big city" are infecting other areas. With each felon committing over 187 felonies per year, the some $430,000 it costs to let one roam free makes the $20,000 per year spent to keep one behind bars seem like a bargain.

Wayne LaPierre, *"Use Laws to Fight Crime, Not Freedom,"* USA Today, March 1, 1989

---

twice before. Forty-five percent have been imprisoned no less than three times and over 20 percent have served more than six previous prison terms. Two-thirds of the prisoners are currently serving sentences for violent crimes, and 84 percent of the other one-third are hardcore repeat offenders, while 6 percent are classified as mentally ill.

Forty-seven percent of all released prisoners are arrested within two years and 40 percent were out on bail, parole, furlough, or probation at the time of arrest. According to the Justice Department, prisoners nationwide serve an average of only 45 percent of their total sentence. . . .

Praying Upon Innocent Citizens

The Justice Department has found that the ratio of commitments to prison to reported serious crimes declined from 1960 to 1986. Professor James Q. Wilson of UCLA notes that "Prisons exist to satisfy our sense of justice and protect us from people who are a menace to society." In today's American society, however, criminals who are found guilty of serious crimes are more likely to be on the streets preying upon innocent citizens than in prison.

The evidence is so overwhelming that it is difficult to understand how anyone can defend the current system. A researcher who tracked the criminal history of every person born in 1958 who lived in Philadelphia from 1968 to 1975 says his study shows the juvenile justice system is too soft on the chronic offender. "We know who he is by the time he is 13 or 14," said Paul E. Tracy, assistant professor of criminal justice at Northwestern University.

Tracy said his findings support the conclusion that more severe punishment would deter juveniles from committing more crime. "My idea is, let's do something about him early and not wait until he's an adult.". . .

A Threat to Public Safety

The majority of felons who are released on probation rather than sent to prison pose a serious threat to public safety, a Rand Corp. study states. The 40-month study, commissioned by the National Institute of Justice, examined 1,672 California felony cases. According to the report, 65 percent of those released were arrested again, 51 percent were convicted of new crimes and 34 percent wound up in jails or prisons. "The repeaters tended to commit burglary, theft, and robbery—the crimes most threatening to public safety," the report said, and about one-third of those convicted were placed on probation again.

"Probation has become the predominant sentencing alternative in this country," the report said. "Sixty to 80 percent of all convicted criminals are sentenced to probation." The Rand research team examined criteria used by courts in sentencing 16,500 convicts in 17 California counties and found that prisons appear to be reserved only for the 232 serious repeat offenders, "career criminals."

While crime skyrockets, our prison population has grown very slowly. Thus, between 1960 and 1985, the rise in total crime (296 percent) was nearly five times as great as the rise in prison population (66 percent), and four times as great as the rise in the numbers sent to prison annually (81 percent). As a result, the chances of a serious crime leading to a prison sentence have fallen from an already slim 3 percent to the current 1 percent.

Crime and Punishment

There has been a clear correlation between the decline in our criminal justice system as a result of Supreme Court decisions on capital punishment and admissible evidence, and the increase in crime. This breakdown began in the 1960s and from 1960 to 1972 serious crime rose from three million reported incidents to eight million—a rise of over 150 percent. During that same period, however, the prison population declined 8 percent—from 212,000 to 196,000. The rate of arrests fell from 18 percent to 14; the rate of imprisonment from 2.6 percent to 1.5.

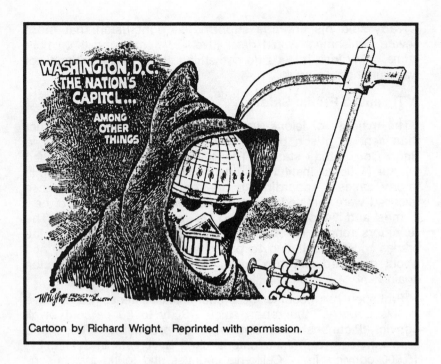

Cartoon by Richard Wright. Reprinted with permission.

That there is a clear relationship between crime and punishment should be beyond question. In the book, *Crime and Human Nature*, Richard J. Herrnstein and James Q. Wilson point out that the 232 percent rise in crime rates from 1960 to 1975 can be explained by the fact that "the rates of most serious crimes went up when the probability of being punished went down."

The relaxation of punishment during these years, say Harvard psychologist Herrnstein and UCLA political scientist Wilson, was "dramatic." They note that between 1960 and 1970 the number of imprisoned offenders decreased from 112 per 100,000 members of the general population to 70. The probability "fell fivefold" that an index crime (included in the FBI-compiled index of reported felonies) "would result in imprisonment."

As the rate dropped, the crime rate soared. Burglaries tripled and robberies more than tripled. Homicide rates rose from 4.7 per 100,000 in 1961 to 10.2 by 1974. Professors Herrnstein and Wilson conclude that many potential criminals, faced with a higher risk of being punished, will find lawful activities relatively more rewarding.

The increase in crime started in the 1960s, a time of great prosperity in which the rewards for non-criminal activity were easily available. The rise in crime, the authors argue, was a rational, predictable response to the reluctance of judges to convict and imprison criminals. By lowering the cost of crime, the judiciary effectively raised its net rewards.

How can we explain the refusal of the American society to punish serious criminals and to subject innocent citizens to the reign of criminal terror we are now witnessing in so many of our urban areas, and even in rural and small-town America?

An Era of Moral Relativism

We seem to believe that criminals are not really responsible for their actions and, as a result, need pay no price for them. Beyond this, in an era of moral relativism, we hesitate to declare any action wrong and immoral, or to confront the existence of evil. Perhaps it is the first sign of a decadent society to reject the value of right and wrong and to fail to distinguish between proper and improper behavior.

Professor Stanley C. Brubaker, of Colgate University states that "There is a point in the history of society when it becomes so pathologically soft and tender that among other things it sides with those who harm it, criminals, and does this quite seriously and honestly. Punishing somehow seems unfair.". . .

The liberal philosophy that criminals are not really responsible for their actions has wreaked havoc upon our society. Professor Murray Rothbard assesses this view in these terms: "Take the case where Smith robs and murders Jones. The old-fashioned view is that Smith is responsible for his act. The modern liberal counters that 'society' is responsible." . . .

If Americans seek to restore safety to our streets and security to our homes and schools, we must restore punishment for crime. We need "truth-in-sentencing," just as we have in labeling for foods. A sentence of 10 years should mean 10 years, and a sentence of life in prison should mean life in prison. Those guilty of violent crime should be removed from society and our criminal justice system should have as its primary goal the protection of innocent law-abiding citizens. The rights of accused criminals should be protected, but one of those "rights" is not a rapid return to the streets to kill or rob or rape again.

If our society will not punish violent crime, and is indifferent to the suffering of innocent victims, what kind of society has ours become? It is within our power to turn our backs upon the decadence which has thrived in legal circles in recent years, and public opinion polls indicate that the vast majority of Americans wish to do so. Making certain that crime is punished swiftly and severely should be the highest priority of local, state and federal officials. Rather than wringing our hands about the escalating rate of violence in our cities, let us finally act to put it to an end.

THE RISE IN URBAN VIOLENCE

GANGS: STAKING CLAIMS ACROSS THE U.S.– AN OVERVIEW

William Robbins

The following reading originally appeared in the New York Times *and was reported from Omaha, Nebraska, by William Robbins. It was later reprinted in the* Star Tribune, *a daily newspaper of the Minneapolis/St. Paul, Minnesota, metropolitan area.*

Points to Consider:

1. Which California gangs are spreading across the United States? Why are they staking claims in other cities?

2. In what ways are these gangs behaving like savvy entrepreneurs? Provide examples to support your answer.

3. How did Minnesota Attorney General Hubert Humphrey propose dealing with gangs?

4. Describe what happened in Omaha when the gangs arrived.

William Robbins, "California Gangs Staking Claims Across the U.S.," *Star Tribune,* December 4, 1988, p. 29A, 33A. Copyright © 1988 by The New York Times Company. Reprinted by permission.

*With the entrepreneurial savvy of MBAs, the '
and Crips are making their way across t'
States, and officials say there are few st.
haven't reached.*

Two California gangs, fanning out along the interstate highway system, are spreading a sophisticated pattern of violence and drug-dealing across the country.

Establishing a Distribution Network

Federal and local law enforcement officials say the gangs have reached east to the Baltimore-Washington, D.C., area, staking out claims along the way in mid-sized cities such as Omaha.

The gangs, the Bloods and the Crips, have abandoned some of the flamboyant hallmarks of their West Coast dealings; they no longer come to town wearing their "colors," a blue bandanna, perhaps, for the Crip or something red for the Blood.

Instead, law enforcement officials say their tactics mimic the entrepreneurial enterprises of newly minted MBAs: They quietly establish a distribution network in markets deemed favorable for the sale of the glut of cocaine and the derivative known as crack that has depressed prices and profits in their own area.

"If you look at a map, you can see the pattern across Middle America," said Michael Shanahan, supervisor of the organized crime unit of the FBI's Kansas City office.

"Just look at the major cities linked together by the interstates and chances are they are there. As they moved out from the home base, each one became a last outpost."

"It's wild," said Sgt. Robert Jackson of the Los Angeles Police Department, who has gained national recognition as an expert on the gangs.

"I would say there are only a few states they haven't reached yet. And the number of places could be in the hundreds."

"Sophisticated Businessmen"

At the Washington headquarters of the FBI, David Binney, chief of the drug section of the criminal investigations division, described the gangs' increasingly methodical operations.

"They do a survey of a city to find out who is doing what there and what the market is," Binney said. "We can use a term like that because they have become very sophisticated businessmen."

JAMAICAN DRUG GANGS

U.S. law enforcement agencies have been calling the Jamaican gangs the most vicious and dangerous organized crime enterprise ever seen in this country.

They're "much more dangerous than the Mafia," according to Stephen E. Higgins, director of the Treasury Department's Bureau of Alcohol, Tobacco and Firearms. . . .

One year ago, federal agents believed that approximately 20 Jamaican posses with about 4,000 members were operating mainly on the East Coast and as far west as Kansas City. Now, according to Higgins, federal agents have identified more than 40 separate posses—with more than 10,000 members—that operate in every part of the United States including Hawaii and Alaska. . . .

Higgins said the posses were armed with the latest in automatic weapons.

Robert J. Wagman, "Drug Threat from Jamaicans Grows," The Milwaukee Journal, July 22, 1988

Police say the Californians began reaching out beyond their Los Angeles borders about two years ago, first moving up the coast to Sacramento, Portland, Seattle and Anchorage.

They moved in, heavily armed, using strong-arm tactics, intimidated any potential opposition and easily undersold their competition.

Law enforcement officials have noticed changes in the style of the gangs' operations over the past few months.

Shanahan said the Crips and Bloods used to make their presence known when they moved into a new city, appearing on the street flaunting expensive jewelry and clothing and renting luxury cars and frequently taking up residence.

"Since July, they have gone underground," Shanahan said. "Often, they carry no identification, and they don't hang around on street corners. They are here to develop a distribution system. They make their contacts, deliver and leave."

No Precise Figures

Law enforcement officials can offer no precise figures on the number of California gang members active outside of their home state.

In Los Angeles County, there are about 70,000 gang members, predominantly blacks but including some Hispanic gangs, according to Lt. Arthur Herrera of the Los Angeles County Sheriff's Department.

Jackson estimates there are 27,000 hard-core gang members in the city of Los Angeles. In California, police say, the Crips outnumber the Bloods by about 3-1.

Gang Activity Throughout the Country

Across the country, estimates reflecting their numbers vary widely, from places such as Denver, where the police estimate gang members now total 700, to St. Louis where Debra Herzog, who heads the region's Drug Enforcement Task Force, a team of federal agents and local police, says a few gang members "are just now establishing themselves."

Minnesota Attorney General Hubert Humphrey last month called drug gangs a major threat to public safety in the state and proposed tougher prison sentences and other measures for organized dealers.

Humphrey said the arrival of the Bloods and Crips gangs makes tougher laws necessary. "These drug gangs are the organized crime families of the 1990s," he said. "They are taking hold in Minnesota. We need the tools and resources to fight them today."

Last summer 15 reputed Los Angeles gang members were arrested shortly after they arrived in Minneapolis/St. Paul to set up drug operations, police said. While law enforcement officials acknowledge that Minneapolis gang activity is less severe than in Los Angeles or Chicago, police say the number of gang members in Minneapolis is growing. Police estimate Minneapolis has 1,500 gang members.

In Omaha, the gang operation is "relatively small," compared with those in other cities, Police Chief Robert Wadman said. But so too, others point out, is the relative size of the city. The police estimate the number of Los Angeles gang members in Omaha at 30.

And though they note that drug sales and violence did not originate with the Bloods and Crips, others observe that levels of violence, the number of arms seized in arrests and the use of crack all have escalated with their arrival in Omaha and with the sharp drop in drug prices that followed.

Robert Armstrong, director of the Omaha Housing Authority, put the problem in human terms.

Cartoon by David Seavey.   Copyright 1989, *USA Today*.   Reprinted with permission.

"All I know is that this year is worse than the year before," he said.   "These people have no fear.   Whether they are Crips or Crip imitators, they sell their drugs any time they feel like selling. And they intimidate the people, make them afraid to call the police, by letting them know they have guns."

THE RISE IN URBAN VIOLENCE

PREVENTION IS THE KEY

Marianne Diaz-Parton

Marianne Diaz-Parton presented the following testimony in her capacity as coastal unit supervisor for Community Youth Gang Services of Los Angeles, California. Ms. Diaz-Parton is also a former gang member.

Points to Consider:

1. Why does prison not serve as punishment for a gang member?

2. Describe Community Youth Gang Services. How does the organization help youth?

3. When did Community Youth Gang Services encounter difficulty in reducing gang violence? What caused this decline in success and why?

4. How many youths has the author been successful in helping? What are the youths doing now?

Excerpted from the testimony of Marianne Diaz-Parton before the House Select Committee on Children, Youth, and Families, March 9, 1988.

There are some gang members who deserve every-thing they get. But the majority are just misguided kids looking for attention, trying to fill the empty spaces, and they need to be worked with and guided by people who really care. Prevention is the key.

My interest in gang activity is very personal. Having lived through it and survived, I'm hoping to do the same for other youth who are going through a very tough time and having to deal with even more violence than I had to. The whole make-up of gangs has changed dramatically. It has gone from the traditional turf wars and mostly street fighting to sophisticated weaponry, drug money, and random killings. I have been most concerned with the youth who have not yet chosen gang membership, and I have done everything I can to prevent that choice.

Lack of Alternatives and Money

As I look around for alternatives, there really aren't that many for our youth. There used to be a time when kids came from two-parent homes, had a school that gave them personal attention, and had activities that kept them out of trouble. A lot of our youth now come from single-parent homes, and those who do not come from a family of two-working parents. Schools have very little time for the gang-involved youth, and would rather kick the youth out of school and try to solve the school's problem rather than solve the youth's problem. I also believe that the community as a whole would rather sweep the problem under the carpet than face the problem head-on and come up with some solutions.

As with anything else, money is the basic need for any program that's going to survive and the money never seems to be there when it comes to saving youth. There are always billions when it comes to saving someone else's country.

The Gang System

I know the reality of facing death head-on and serving time in the federal penitentiary for gang activity. There was no form of rehabilitation in the penitentiary. In fact, had it not been for some very concerned people, one being a deputy sheriff from

---

LOS ANGELES STREET GANGS

Essie Love, a social worker from Watts, shudders every time she sees yellow ribbons in her neighborhood.

Police string up the yellow bands to rope off homicide scenes. In the troubled turf where she lives and works, the victims too often are children killed in gang-related violence.

"The parents lose one child to the gangs and grieve. We counselors lose a child every week," the veteran counselor for Community Youth Gang Services said. "Sometimes it's almost too much to bear."

Street gang killings in Los Angeles, the nation's second largest city, are up nearly 25 percent, to the highest level in six years. Gang membership reportedly has increased by more than 10,000 since 1980.

Police blame the killings on drug traffic, saying some gangs fight over profits. Community leaders point to poverty and racism.

Dennis Anderson, *"Gangs Have Spawned Crime, Fear and Death on Los Angeles Streets,"* Star Tribune, *March 7, 1987*

Lennox,* I may have come out more hardened and crazier than when I went in. The gang activity is more condensed and aggressive in the penitentiary, and it does not serve as a punishment for youth; it gives them the stripes in their neighborhoods that give them some respect.

The gang runs on a system very similar to most businesses. They have management, middle management, steering committees and employees, and everyone trying to get to the top. That happens through violence.

Community Youth Gang Services

Youth Gang Services has been struggling for six years through budget cuts, through people saying how unorthodox we are, and through some politicians wondering how they can allow ex-felons and ex-gang members to go out and try to re-direct

---

*Editor's note: Lennox is an unincorporated area of Los Angeles County.

our youth. My answer to that is an alcoholic doesn't want to be talked to by someone who's never been there, and a Vietnam veteran doesn't want to hear from a psychologist how to deal with his problems. A gang member wants to be talked to by someone who understands from the heart, from experience, and from caring; not from some forced court order. I don't understand why the country, the state, or anyone else didn't jump on this problem in its infancy. Why did they wait until we had all-out wars on our streets, and why did they wait until some non-gang territories were being frequented by gang members? Why did people wait until then to try to put a stop to it?

The organization I work for employs just under 500 streetwise counselors to deal with approximately 500,000 gang members. I call this a Band-Aid on a severed arm. It seems to me it is destined to fail. Our agency is constantly trying to do things without the resources to do them, but we were successful in reducing gang violence until 1984 when cocaine came into the picture. Traditional gang violence was something that could be dealt with on a gang level, and we were successful. But when you start talking about thousands and millions of dollars that have been inaccessible in the past to our youth, it is almost impossible to convince them that gaining some of the material things that every American wants is not right. The fancy cars, cellular phones, gold, money are very alluring to kids on the street. Drug dealers know this. And they prey on our youth and profit by them.

Misguided Kids

Gang members are perfect targets. They are already organized, they have been turned down by every traditional way of earning money because of their color, the possibility of their being a gang member, and their past criminal record. They find it easier to go to "the main man" and make a few hundred a day, even if it means possible imprisonment, injury, or death. Gang warfare has become more sophisticated because of the ability to buy sophisticated weaponry. We now deal with automatic weapons, Uzis, and grenades. They buy all this with drug money. They also acquire weapons through people who are strung out on cocaine and who commit robberies and burglaries. These people bring weapons they have used in crimes and trade them for whatever cocaine the gang members will give up.

Illustration by Craig MacIntosh. Reprinted by permission of *Star Tribune, Newspaper of the Twin Cities*.

I believe that law enforcement is a needed force in the community, and that they need to target the drug dealers. Also, there are some gang members who deserve everything they get. But the majority are just misguided kids looking for attention, trying to fill the empty spaces, and they need to be worked with and guided by people who really care. The kids can see through a fake, and they will clam up. I know it's possible because someone cared about me. I felt it in my heart. And I am where I am today because of that person.

Prevention Is the Key

I have been successful with at least 50 youths. They're the ones who keep me going in this job, telling me that if it weren't for us and the time we put into them as people, and not as hoodlums, as a lot of people like to call them. I have gang members who are now in the service, owning their own business, counseling youth as I do, and some going into the police academy. It took a lot of convincing, wheeling and dealing with officials to let them get that far, but we can't scrap all our youth and put them in one category and say we're going to wipe out youth gangs.

Prevention is the key. Schools need to hire people who are capable of counseling these youth, counseling the teachers, counseling the parents, and bringing people to understand that giving up on these kids is giving up on the future. I hope you never have to look in your backyard and see the problem creeping into your part of town and killing somebody close to you, because bullets don't have a name on them and when they start flying they don't stop until they hit something.

9   THE RISE IN URBAN VIOLENCE

GANGS CANNOT BE ABOLISHED

Robert Allen

Robert Allen is a former gang leader. He presented the following testimony in his capacity as an assistant to the House of UMOJA in Philadelphia, Pennsylvania, a community-based program for young gang members that was founded and is directed by Sister Falaka Fattah. House of UMOJA attempts to intervene in the lives of gang members.

Points to Consider:

1. Explain why the author believes gangs cannot be abolished.

2. The author says that putting gang members in jail does not work. Why not?

3. Summarize the author's experience at the House of UMOJA. How has he been able to assist gang members? What has he done with his life since he met Sister Fattah?

Excerpted from the testimony of Robert Allen before the House Select Committee on Children, Youth, and Families, March 9, 1988.

Since I was part of the problem, I'm going to always try to be part of the solution now. . . . But we cannot get rid of the gangs.

A gang is a family, no doubt about it. Anybody who thinks he can stop gangs is just wasting his time. The thing is not to stop the gangs; it's to stop the negativity of the gangs. Gangs are a positive thing if they are doing it in a positive way. The great unity that black people have is gangs. The only problem they have is that they do violent harm against each other. . . .

Working with Gangs

I've been to Los Angeles, Chicago, Atlanta, and many other cities. I've worked with different gangs: the Savage Nomads, the Ching-a-lings, the Black Stone Rangers, the Almighty, and they all have the same problems.

If you are going to fight the gangs, you cannot sit here and tell a gang that you are going to try to battle them. You have to sit here and tell them you are going to try to work with them and come up with some solutions. You cannot ask any gangs to stop if you're not going to have a solution. . . .

Problems in the Schools

The problem with the schools is you took the discipline out, getting child abuse mixed up with discipline. You have to discipline children. Now, any time a child knows that he cannot be disciplined he's going to act up. He's going to do what he wants to do. So, you have to come up with some kind of solution where a child cannot tell a teacher, "If you hit me, I'm going to put you on charges of child abuse."

Now, it's up to the child to learn. The teacher cannot make him learn. I gang-warred for ten years. The teachers told me I wouldn't live to be 18. I'm 34. So, every year I go back to the high school and let them know I'm here another year, and I've gone to college for five years. I know if I wouldn't have met Sister Fattah in 1972, I probably would be dead or in the penitentiary for the rest of my live.

What I'm saying is that nobody in any city or any state can fight any gang. The best thing to do is try to work along with them. You have to tell them not to be like you were, but to be like you are now. Every young gang member has somebody that was his idol from the past and he's trying to be like that person. So, you have to take your time and sit down and say,

A SENSE OF BELONGING

U.S. gang life had its genesis in the Northeast of the 1840s, particularly in the depressed neighborhoods of Boston and New York where young Irishmen developed gangs to sustain social solidarity and to forge a collective identity based on common ethnic roots. Since then, youth of every ethnic and racial origin have formed gangs for similar reasons, and at times have even functioned to protect their own ethnic or racial group from attack by harmful outsiders. Overall, a persistent reason for joining gangs is the sense of absolute belonging and unsurpassed social love that results from gang membership. Especially for young black men whose lives are at a low premium in America, gangs have fulfilled a primal need to possess a sense of social cohesion through group identity. Particularly when traditional avenues for the realization of personal growth, esteem, and self-worth, usually gained through employment and career opportunities, have been closed, young black men find gangs a powerful alternative.

Gangs also offer immediate material gratification through a powerful and lucrative underground economy. This underground economy is supported by exchanging drugs and services for money, or by barter. The lifestyle developed and made possible by the sale of crack presents often irresistible economic alternatives to young black men frustrated by their own unemployment. The death that can result from involvement in such drug- and gang-related activity is ineffective in prohibiting young black men from participating.

Michael Dyson, "The Plight of Black Men," Zeta, February 1989

"don't be like we were, be like we are now."

Cocaine: The Poor Man's High

Cocaine used to be a rich man's high and now it's a poor man's high. What public welfare needs to do is start checking on these welfare people who trade these food stamps in for cocaine and spend their checks on cocaine instead of feeding their children and paying their bills.

You should go around when they get their food stamps and

check the refrigerators and see whose refrigerators are filled and whose are empty and you'll know who is on drugs. When young kids come home with gold on all their fingers and all around their necks, then the parent in that house is condoning their behavior because they have to know what they're doing.

Jail Does Not Work

Now, I've heard people say that they should be locked up. All young people shouldn't be locked up. A lot of them are misdirected. So, what you should do is not allow them to go through the juvenile system a hundred times. When they come there three times then that's when you're going to have to put your foot down and deal with them. If you let them go through there a hundred times, of course, they're going to keep on doing it and think they can get over. Somebody is going to have to deal with them right then and there. Don't say "Lock them up" because if you lock some of them up, then they get institutionalized and then they use that to their advantage. For instance, when I went to jail, one thing I found was that all the gangs that we were fighting stuck together. If we were from West Philly, we stuck together. If we were from North Philly, we stuck together. If we were from South Philly, we stuck together. So, I said to myself, "If I can do that in here, I'm going back out on the street and do it."

Nobody ever told me what a human life meant. Until I met Sister Fattah, I didn't care about shooting or killing anybody. Then she told me only God is supposed to take a human life. You've also got to get these churches more involved. When I was younger, the reverends would get out there on the street with us and walk with us and talk with us and go to the police station with us. They don't do that any more.

Young people need to realize that there are people out there who are trying to make money off them, who want them to gang fight, who want them to kill. But then you give money to programs that are not working. You should have some young people sitting right up there with you making decisions for young people. Ask them which programs are working, which programs should get funded.

House of UMOJA: More Than a Paycheck

At House of UMOJA, we don't get paid. . . .every month, every week, we're dealing with a gang problem that other people are getting paid for. We have one thing they don't. A young life means more to us than a paycheck. That's what a lot of other

Illustration by David Seavey. Copyright 1984, *USA Today*. Reprinted with permission.

people have to start doing, stop thinking about that paycheck and getting paid and think about saving one of those kid's lives. You save one out of a hundred and that's worth more than a million dollars.

I wish that you would get some kind of group that would bring their resources together and just go to different cities and help each other out. That's all we could do. But we cannot get rid of the gangs. . . .

So, you have to work with the parents and the young people. I just thank God that they sent Sister Fattah before I got killed or went to jail for the rest of my life. She helped me go on to college for five years. She showed me that I had leadership potential to use in a positive way, not a negative way. So, since

I was part of the problem, I'm going to always try to be part of the solution now. Because there's going to always be young people killing young people.

10 THE RISE IN URBAN VIOLENCE

MORE COMMITTED SOCIAL SERVICES ARE NEEDED

Elliott Currie

Professor Elliott Currie presented the following testimony in his capacity as a criminologist at the Center for the Study of Law and Society, University of California-Berkeley. Dr. Currie has been studying youth violence for over 20 years.

Points to Consider:

1. How has the economic situation of recent years affected lower-income families? Please be specific in your answer.

2. Why have public agencies and public schools been of little help to these families?

3. Explain why the juvenile justice system has become the social service agency of first choice for these families.

4. What suggestions does the author offer to help violent youth?

Excerpted from the testimony of Elliott Currie before the House Select Committee on Children, Youth, and Families, March 9, 1988.

We need serious and adequately funded family resource programs. . . . And much more. We don't lack for things to do or useful models. What we lack, so far, is will and commitment.

During the past year I've been engaged in a study of the roots of violence, hard-drug abuse, and self-destructive behavior among kids in one American urban community. I've been talking in depth with several dozen young people, many of them locked up in juvenile institutions. They are black, white, and Hispanic, male and female; what they have in common is serious trouble—and the fact that most of them are products of some very destructive social and economic forces which have now been underway for some time.

Children of Economic Disaster

Most of the young people I've been working with are, first and foremost, the children of the economic disaster that's afflicted the poorest 25 or 30 percent of the American population over the past 15 years. They were born just about the time when the fortunes of the lower-income family—never very promising—began to shift downward. . . . Let me just remind you of the extent of the disaster that's affected many of these families in recent years. Since 1974, about the time the youngest of the kids I've talked with were born, the share of income going to the poorest fifth of the population has fallen by about 20 percent. In real dollars, the income of poor families with young children has fallen by 25 percent in the past decade. There were 2.5 million more poor kids under 18 in 1985 than just six years earlier.

All of these numbers get pretty abstract, to the point where we are numbed by them after awhile. But they come alive, believe me, when you talk to troubled and violent kids in the flesh. These are kids whose parents have lost good jobs, or never had them, in the wake of the de-industrialization that's ravaged the labor markets of the cities since the early 1970s. Some of them are parents who have never worked and who, perhaps, never will. Others, casualties of the same economic trends, may be working two or even three low-wage jobs in order to put together an income sufficient to keep them from being evicted and to buy their kids enough decent clothes so they won't feel humiliated at school.

┌───┐

THE UNDERLYING ISSUE

The epidemic of gang-related violence that has hit this country is shocking.

Prepare for further shocks.

In Washington, D.C., Los Angeles, New York, and other communities across the nation, armed warfare is becoming a common response to the irritations of daily life—business deals gone awry, arguments with family members, envy over a neighbor's new leather jacket or designer sunglasses.

From 1984 to 1986, the rate of violence among youth rose 9 percent nationwide, a reversal of the decline of the past decade. To date, we have attempted to quell this upsurge with police crackdowns. But while police action may clear the streets for a few days, gang members brag that they easily adapt their operations and continue as before. It is obvious that law enforcement, while essential, is not the answer to youth violence. If we want to stop children from killing each other, we must address a much tougher underlying issue—the neighborhoods they call home.

It comes as no surprise that the highest incidence of crime occurs in communities where the supporting structures of school, job, and family have come undone. Children growing up in our poorest neighborhoods are far more likely to fare poorly in school, become teenage mothers, suffer chronic unemployment and resort to crime and violence. They grow up with little investment in their future, and little evidence from their bleak environment that the future is something worth investing in. When they pull a gun and risk a jail term, they have little future to risk.

George Miller, *"Ending Gangs Will Require Effort by All,"* Milwaukee Journal

Lack of Social Supports

But the economic disaster that's hit so many of these families isn't just a matter of not having enough dollars. Perhaps even more importantly, it has accelerated the breakup of the social supports that might help these families bring up their kids in humane and compassionate ways. The families of these kids are always moving—nobody ever seems to live in the same place for long. A startling number of my kids were born somewhere else than where they're living—in a different state, different city, different neighborhood. So the family is constantly uprooted, losing friends, extended kin, other stable and respected adults to help care for the children, provide role models, and generally ease the burdens of work and childrearing. They move to find a better job—or any job—or to find cheaper housing because they've lost a job and/or the rent has gone up beyond what they can afford. So in addition to the economic strain these families suffer is a deeper and perhaps even more destructive social impoverishment and isolation.

Faced with this, many families manage to do surprisingly well. But others, perhaps those more vulnerable to begin with, simply collapse—collapse into passivity and disability, into alcohol and hard-drug abuse, into routine violence against their children. The level of drug use among some of the parents of the kids I've talked with, in particular, is simply astonishing. They may start by using drugs to get through the day, especially if they're working two or more jobs. But sometimes the drugs gain control; the parent pretty much ceases to function altogether, and the child winds up paying the bills and doing the grocery shopping—if it's done at all.

The Weakening of Public Agencies

The isolation and social and economic impoverishment among these families is compounded by the weakening of the *public* agencies of support and care. Again, there are plenty of figures charting the extent of cutbacks in public social services, in Medicaid, in community mental health services, in drug treatment. But when you see the reality at close range, it is startling. I often ask kids a question that goes something like this: when you had a problem or got in trouble, or your mom started to smoke rock cocaine, or you were getting beat up at home, was there anybody to help? Usually the answer is "no." For the families of these children there are shockingly few public services that they can afford or that have the resources to make any effort at outreach to families in need of help. Paradoxically and tragically, families that are more "together" or have more resources can generally find decent family support services, psychological help, adequate drug treatment; the families that most need them cannot.

"Sink or Swim"

That same tragic process—in which the young who are favored with more resources can get still more while those less favored are left to flounder and sink—also infects the public

Illustration by David Seavey. Copyright 1985, *USA Today*. Reprinted with permission.

schools. In talking with troubled kids I've heard of some very good experiences with school, some effective and caring teachers. But more often the school, in the "sink or swim" society these kids increasingly face, is a place of humiliation, defeat, and festering resentment. All too often, the schools—especially those with a high proportion of low-income kids—are institutions that are less devoted to teaching the young than, in a sense, to validating, or ranking, them according to the pre-existing abilities they bring to the school. If they have the familial or intellectual resources already, the public schools may serve them very well indeed. But heaven help the kid, in many public schools today, who enters with a learning disability or a behavior problem. I can't tell you how many of the young people I've talked with began their journey to the juvenile justice system this way—with a school problem that caused them to slip out of school virtually unnoticed, or get thrown out. But the result is catastrophic for a kid today, for in the last quarter of the twentieth century in the United States there is virtually nothing respectable—or legal—for a kid of 16 years old to do all day long outside of high school.

The Juvenile Justice System

The erosion of the public sector means that there is shockingly little constructive intervention in the lives of most of the kids I've talked with. So emotional or medical problems go untreated, family violence or parental addiction unnoticed or, if noticed, inadequately addressed. For many of these families and their children, the juvenile justice system has increasingly become the social service agency of first resort—the only way they can be assured of getting basic services is by getting locked up. I've often seen concerned police or probation workers incarcerate a kid just to ensure that he or she gets a couple of nutritious meals every day, basic medical services, and someone to keep them from hurting themselves or damaging their brains with chemicals, at least for the time being. But, of course, without some deeper intervention, the underlying problems are left unresolved. The result is that the juvenile justice system becomes a revolving door; the same faces appear over and over from one year to the next, and the kids are, for the most part, unafraid of it and increasingly contemptuous of it—and often bitterly angry and resentful over the way it treats them. For some kids, in fact, the threat of prison backfires; one 17-year-old crack dealer—female—told me that, after money, the second reason kids were attracted to dealing dope was the respect others gave you knowing that you were courting hard prison time.

It's terribly clear that the roots of youthful violence are many and tangled, and because we've left them alone—or aggravated them—for so long, have deepened. But there are a number of things we can and must do, and the encouraging part is that we know how to do them. . . .

We Need Committed Programs

Two areas are especially critical and have been under siege in recent years: work and family. In stressing the importance of work, I'm not saying that we need more jobs for kids. There are already a lot of those; most of the kids I've been working with have been in and out of the teenage labor market; they'll work at Taco Bell for awhile and then quit, often alternating that with selling dope. What they do *not* have in our current economy is the prospect of a more challenging work role in the future, an adult livelihood that's worth looking forward to, that's sufficiently compelling to keep them in school in a serious way and off of the dope track. When I ask kids what they'd really like to do in the future they either say they don't know or they want to be famous professional athletes or movie stars. What's deeply, tragically missing in their view of the future is any concrete vision of how they'd contribute to a recognizable adult community and be respected for it. Without that vision I really don't see an alternative, for many kids, to the pull of the dope trade and its attendant violence. The kids who are serious drug dealers aren't afraid of whatever we might throw at them by way of imprisonment, and they'll say, at least in public, that they're not afraid of getting hurt or killed in the line of business. "You're gonna die someday," they'll tell you; "you're gonna die young or you're gonna die old." Meanwhile, if you're brave and smart you can live very well indeed; as one crack dealer I've gotten to know likes to say, "who have heart, have money."

We also need serious and adequately funded family resource programs. . . . The families of violent kids need help in many intertwined ways, and most of all help in raising their children without the use of violence. I've always believed there was a connection between violent families and violent kids. But I've still been amazed at what I've seen this year. Almost without exception the volatile kids I've talked with come from families where violence against the child was the norm. No matter if they were black, white, or Hispanic, these kids talk with bitterness and anger about "whuppin'," about the "belt." It's hard to stop parents from hurting children without also working to relieve the larger pressures the economy and the weakened public sector have placed on them. But we can start. And we know how.

There is much more. We need to replace the current rhetorical war on drugs with real treatment, complete with aggressive outreach and aftercare for the vast numbers of children — and parents — who need it. We need to restore resources for accessible health care, to ward off remediable damage from untreated health problems or poor prenatal care. We need serious commitment to addressing learning problems in the public schools, in caring and humane ways. Of course, we need sufficient and high-quality day care. And much more. We don't lack for things to do or useful models. What we lack, so far, is will and commitment.

70

A Challenge to Our Culture

Shortly before I was asked to come to this hearing, I spent the better part of an afternoon with a 15-year-old crack dealer behind bars for having beaten a man nearly to death over an eight-dollar drug misunderstanding. Over and over again, he kept repeating that where he lived, "only the strong survive." And I thought, yes, he's right—at least, enough right to be deeply troubling. The bottom line in understanding the current tragedy of youth violence is that we've created a society in which, at the bottom, it takes strength, or cunning, or sheer good luck to survive, at least with a measure of dignity or self-esteem. But in a society where there are fewer and fewer legitimate options for the energetic, and not much help for those who start out hobbled or who weaken or stumble along the way, being strong may come to mean being willing to maim (or to kill) someone for eight dollars. Ultimately this is a challenge to our culture at its deepest levels.

11 THE RISE IN URBAN VIOLENCE

DEALING WITH EVIL

George Will

George Will, a nationally syndicated columnist, also makes frequent television and magazine commentary.

Points to Consider:

1. Describe the Central Park "wilding."

2. What theories have experts offered to explain the "wilding"? What reason did the boys offer?

3. How should society deal with evil?

George Will, "Why Can We See No Evil Where Evil Is Real?" *St. Paul Pioneer-Press Dispatch,* April 30, 1989. © 1989, Washington Post Writers Group. Reprinted with permission.

We have lost the ability to speak the language of emphatic judgment.

"There seem," says a professor described as a specialist in adolescent behavior, "to have been some socioeconomic factors involved." Ah.

Here is what those "factors" were "involved" in.

Central Park "Wilding"

More than 30 boys, most under 16, went "wilding." In their rampage, they raped and battered nearly to death a 28-year-old jogger in Central Park near Harlem. They hit her with a pipe, hacked her skull and thighs with a knife, pounded her face with a brick, bound her hands beneath her chin with her bloody sweatshirt, which also served as a gag. Seven or more boys raped her. (One boy says he "only played with the lady's legs" and another says he only felt her breasts and held her down while others raped her.)

Her larynx may have been crushed. She lay undiscovered for nearly four hours, losing three-quarters of her blood. The puddle she lay in hastened hypothermia and her temperature fell to 80.

Expert Opinions

Various experts say they know why this happened. Alienation, anomie, boredom, rage—raging boredom?—peer pressure, inequality, status anxieties, television, advertising.

The professor who says "there seem to have been some socioeconomic factors involved" elaborates: "The media, especially television, is constantly advertising these various things that are necessary to define yourself, to be an acceptable person, and the joggers may represent a level of socioeconomic attainment that the media has convinced everybody is necessary to be an acceptable person. So, to that extent, such people become a target." Ah.

Science of Victimology

Who is the victim? Well, yes, of course, the woman. But her identity, even her reality, disappears as she recedes into a category: high attainers. The boys, too, are victims. They were provoked by high attainers and disoriented by media-imposed criteria of acceptable personhood.

We have here another triumph of the social science of

WILDING

The word "wilding" is new, but the conduct it signifies is as old as human sin. One heinous example is the recent attack on a young woman, who was jogging in New York's Central Park, by a pack of juveniles. The magazine, U.S. NEWS, reports:

"The attackers were children wielding rocks and pipes. . . Spotting a woman on the jogging path, they set upon her, beating and raping her and leaving her for dead . . .The jailed teenagers joked and laughed about their deeds, singing a rap song called 'Wild Thing'." (May 8, 1989, page 10)

The politicians and pundits of the press are crying out in bewilderment, "why?". Their usual rationalizations to excuse inexcusable conduct are inadequate. . . .

The truth is that all human beings are born with a sinful nature and are capable of the most bestial actions. The Bible teaches that all are fallen sinful beings. Freud, no Bible lover, teaches also that destructive aggression is inherent in human nature.

Fred Schwarz, *"Wilding,"* Christian Anti-Communism Crusade, *June 1, 1989*

victimology. Its specialty is the universalization of victimhood, the dispersal of responsibility into a fog of "socioeconomic factors."

"On the other hand," says the professor, "that doesn't explain why they would attack a homeless person." A homeless person was one of the "wilding" pack's eight victims before they caught the woman.

The fact that the *New York Times* considers the professor an illuminating source is itself illuminating. It reveals the rhetoric that elite liberal institutions find convincing and comforting when confronted by horror.

More Theories

Another theorist is heard from: "One doesn't have to excuse sociopathic behavior to notice the contrast of visible, great wealth and massive poverty." Verily, nail your political agenda to every passing tragedy: The "lesson" here is to "do something" about the "underclass." First, of course, a task force.

Never mind the fact that most of the attackers come from comfortable middle- or working-class homes. Four live in a building with a doorman.

Another theorist speaks of the boys' "unfocused rage." The frequent references to the attackers' "rage" are fascinating because there is not a scintilla of evidence of rage. Actually, one of the boys blurted out the reason they did it. The reason he gave is theoretically unsatisfying, politically unuseful and philosophically unsettling, so he will not be heard: "It was something to do. It was fun."

Newspaper reports have repeatedly referred to the "wilding" attacks as "motiveless." But fun is a motive. Policemen, with their knack of the language of unvarnished fact, refer to "wildings"—packs of boys looting stores and inflicting random beatings—as a "pastime." Pastimes are adopted for fun.

In earlier, simpler—or were they?—days, descriptions of an episode like the one in Central Park would have begun with a judgment that today is never reached at all: The attackers did what they did because they are evil.

Personal Evil

Today people respond: "Evil? such a primitive notion—not at all useful as an explanation." But that response is not real sophistication, it is a form of flinching. It is a failure of nerve. A vanishing moral vocabulary is being replaced by academic rubbish collected reflexively by "serious" newspapers. They serve up a rich sauce of sociological cant that coats reality, making it unrecognizable.

We have lost the ability to speak the language of emphatic judgment. As James Q. Wilson says, "Our habits of the heart have been subverted by the ambitions of the mind."

The ambition of the modern mind is to spare itself a chilling sight, that of the cold blank stare of personal evil. The modern program is squeamishness dressed up as sophistication. Its aim is to make the reality of evil disappear behind a rhetorical gauze of learned garbage.

Until relatively recently in most societies, people who did what the "wilding" boys did would have been punished swiftly and with terrible severity.

Punishment in this case will be interminably delayed and ludicrously light. The boys know that; that is one reason they were singing rap songs in their jail cells.

A society that flinches from the fact of evil will flinch from the act of punishment. It should not wonder why it does not feel safe.

RESTRICT WAR WEAPONS

Glenn McNatt

Glenn McNatt originally wrote this article for The Baltimore Evening Sun.

Points to Consider:

1. How do assault weapons differ from ordinary hunting rifles?

2. What countries export assault weapons to the United States? Do these countries permit their own citizens to possess such weapons?

3. Why does the United States tolerate the sale of assault weapons?

4. Is there a contradiction between Israel and West Germany's weapon sales? Please explain your answer.

Glenn McNatt, "Assault-gun Suppliers No Friends to America," *Star Tribune,* February 3, 1989. Reprinted by permission of *The Baltimore Evening Sun.*

Any trade partner that deliberately floods the U.S. civilian market with powerful, paramilitary weapons that it would never for a moment consider allowing its own citizens to own cannot be considered wholly friendly.

Last month a deranged man wielding an AK-47 assault rifle shot and killed five children and wounded 30 others outside a Stockton, California, elementary school before taking his own life. The incident has prompted a rising chorus of demands to ban such weapons.

Assault Weapons

Unlike ordinary hunting rifles and shotguns, military-type assault weapons typically are capable of firing dozens of rounds without reloading. The schoolyard gunman in Stockton was able to squeeze off 70 shots in less than a minute. Most assault weapons fire large-caliber, high-velocity military ammunition that makes them of limited use for sportsmen.

Yet sales of such weapons have risen sharply in recent years, thanks in part to an aggressive marketing campaign waged by the manufacturers through the specialized gun press. Assault rifles such as the Soviet-designed Kalishnikov AK-47, exported by China, the Israeli Uzi submachine gun and the American Colt AR-15R, a derivative of the M-16 rifle used by American troops in Vietnam, are the latest craze featured in the pages of such magazines as *Guns & Ammo.*

All of those weapons were originally developed for their country's respective armed forces in military or antiterrorist operations. In order to be sold legally in the United States, the manufacturers must modify them from fully automatic operation, which permits the weapon to fire continuously as long as the trigger is depressed, to semiautomatic, which requires a separate pull of the trigger for each shot.

Personal Freedom

Those who buy and sell assault rifles say that the issue is one of personal freedom. Gun dealers report that most of the people who purchase such weapons use them for weekend plinking at tin cans.

It is ironic, however, that none of the countries exporting military-style assault rifles to the United States permit their own citizens unlimited right to possess such weapons. West

---

ASSAULT WEAPONS AND CRIME

An assault gun is 20 times more likely than a conventional firearm to be used in crime, according to a study by Cox Newspapers.

While assault guns account for less than one out of 200 privately owned guns in the United States, they were used in one of 10 crimes that resulted in a firearms trace last year, the study shows.

The findings appear to document for the first time what police have been saying for months: that semiautomatic guns patterned after military firearms are the favored weapon of a growing number of criminals, especially violence-prone drug gangs in larger U.S. cities.

"Study Finds Criminals Favor Semiautomatic Weapons," Star Tribune, May 21, 1989

Germany, the Eastern Bloc countries and China, for example, all severely restrict the possession of firearms by private individuals. Israel issues Uzi submachine guns to Jewish settlers in the occupied territories but makes the possession of similar firearms by Arabs a serious crime.

America's Unique Tolerance

In fact, the United States is probably the only country in the world that allows private citizens to own what are essentially military weapons. Were it not for America's unique tolerance, there would be virtually no market for the types of weapons being exported by the Chinese and the Israelis. Presumably the tolerance stems, at least in part, from American efforts to strengthen trade ties with those two nations.

Yet any trade partner that deliberately floods the U.S. civilian market with powerful, paramilitary weapons that it would never for a moment consider allowing its own citizens to own cannot be considered wholly friendly.

A Contradiction

Recently, for example, the Israelis were outraged by reports that a West German company had sold Libya materials that could be used to manufacture chemical weapons. Israeli commentators roundly criticized the West German government

Illustration by Craig MacIntosh. Reprinted by permission of *Star Tribune, Newspaper of the Twin Cities.*

for allowing the sale of potentially deadly agents to a country that has been denounced as a terrorist state.

Somehow the commentators saw no contradiction between Germans selling nerve gas in Tripoli and Israelis selling Uzi submachine guns in Detroit. Both nations undoubtedly would claim that they were purely commercial transactions for which they bore no moral responsibility.

If instead of making fertilizer the Libyans used German chemicals to manufacture weapons with which to slaughter villagers in neighboring Chad, that's no concern of the company that sold them the materials. Similarly, if dope dealers in Detroit employ Uzi submachine guns to take out the competition—along with any innocent bystanders caught in the cross fire—well, you can't make an omelet without breaking eggs.

With friends like that, who needs enemies?

13   THE RISE IN URBAN VIOLENCE

BANNING WEAPONS IS THE REAL MENACE

National Rifle Association

The National Rifle Association (NRA), founded in 1871, is an independent, nonprofit organization devoted to the safe and efficient use of small arms for recreation and protection. It has long been a leader in the opposition to gun-control legislation. The NRA is financially supported by its approximately 3 million members.

Points to Consider:

1. Why should all firearms owners be concerned about the calls for banning semi-automatic firearms?

2. What is the familiar anti-gun "bait and switch" technique?

3. According to the NRA, how should society deal with crime?

4. Describe the NRA's six crime-fighting initiatives.

Excerpted from a National Rifle Association (NRA) pamphlet on semi-automatic firearms and from NRA testimony on assault weapons.

All firearms owners should beware. Those who would willingly sacrifice handguns as a compromise, and who may now be willing to sacrifice semi-automatic firearms, will eventually find themselves having to defend their shotguns or any other type of firearm they choose to own.

Semi-automatic firearms are used extensively by millions of citizens throughout America – bird hunters, water-fowlers, competitive shooters, and collectors.

Semi-automatic rifles, shotguns, and pistols are nothing new, employing basic designs that date from the turn-of-the-century. Their distinctive feature is that after firing a single shot by one pull of the trigger, a mechanism reloads another cartridge for firing. The mechanism is simply equivalent to, and sometimes *slower* than, some other commonly used methods of providing additional shots. For instance, some pump shotguns can be fired more rapidly than semi-automatics.

The Citizen's Choice

Current legislative proposals to ban the sale, ownership, and possession of semi-automatic firearms are uninformed and misdirected at best, and represent clear dangers to all law-abiding American gun owners.

The national media and organized "gun control" groups have advanced from demanding prohibitions on certain handguns and ammunition, to calls for banning semi-automatic firearms. The pattern is obvious, and the strategy has long been clear – isolate certain types of firearms, label them as inherently "evil" or "crime prone," then try to segregate and drive a wedge between firearms owners.

All firearms owners should beware. Those who would willingly sacrifice handguns as a compromise, and who may now be willing to sacrifice semi-automatic firearms, will eventually find themselves having to defend their shotguns or any other type of firearm they choose to own. . . .

Stopping the Wheels of Progress

It is ironic and the very height of hypocrisy that gun prohibitionists who deliberately misinterpret the Second Amendment "right to keep and bear arms" by claiming it limits the right solely for militia purposes (i.e., National Guard) and not for individuals, now seek to ban semi-automatic firearms

THE SECOND AMENDMENT

The Second Amendment to our Constitution was not conceived and ratified in the interest of "sport" or "recreation." It was—and is—guarantee to individuals that they will have a "sporting chance" at self-protection, or to avert tyranny if the occasion ever arises.

Dan Warrensford, *"Such a Weapons Ban Is the Real Menace,"* USA Today, January 23, 1989

because they *are allegedly suitable or convertible for military use.*

Keep in mind that the U.S. military still uses muzzleloaders for ceremonial purposes, still uses airguns and .22 caliber pistols and rifles for training, still uses bolt-action center-fire rifles for sniping, still uses pump-action and semi-automatic shotguns for guard, patrol, training and recreational purposes, still uses many types of revolvers and semi-automatic pistols plus full- and semi-automatic rifles for defense, offense and training. In short, they use every type of gun, and that's exactly what Handgun Control, Inc., and the National Coalition to Ban Handguns are after. . . .

Semi-Autos Under Assault

Using the familiar anti-gun "bait and switch" technique, the definition of so-called "assault rifles" can be changed at will by proponents of legislation to affect virtually any rifle (or shotgun or pistol) that can fit into the fluid definition. In the same manner, under some bills, the definition of "cop-killer bullets" would have covered 85 percent of hunting rounds and "Saturday Night Specials" would have been expandable to all handguns.

Although some shotgunners think the current legislative push against the semi-auto rifles and pistols won't affect them, that's not true. The semi-automatic shotgun and the pump action can be converted to full-auto, and the pump action can be fired faster than the semi-automatic even without conversion. The double-barrel shotgun can be made to discharge both barrels at one pull of the trigger, making it arguably a full auto.

Some riflemen feel that their pump actions or lever actions or bolt-actions won't be affected. They forget that all these types have been and can be converted to full-auto.

Some revolver shooters feel confident that their guns will be in no more jeopardy than usual. But the Webley-Fosbery was a revolver "turned into a semi-auto" and the Union Arms revolver had a selective-fire potential. Further, the famed Ed McGivern accurately and regularly fired conventional revolvers at *machine gun* speed.

Under most legislative schemes proposed, firearms would be classified as "assault-type" if the firearm looks like a military firearm and if "the firearm can be readily converted from semi-automatic to fully automatic."

The design and readily convertible tests are ambiguous and could ultimately be used by the Bureau of Alcohol, Tobacco and Firearms (BATF) at the federal level or agencies at the state level to label and outlaw virtually all semi-automatic rifles and pistols as "assault weapons.". . .

Punish Criminals, Not Law-Abiding Citizens

Attempting to legislate against semi-automatic firearms on the basis of design features is a false issue. It's like arguing that all firearms should be restricted because they might be used or be altered to be used in a crime. The basic, underlying premise of all gun control that "guns cause crime," or that there are "good" firearms and "bad" firearms, defies common sense.

Whether a firearm is long or short barreled, fires a single or multiple rounds, its capability for "good" or "evil" rests solely in the hands of its owner. The true test of any firearm, be it muzzleloader or of automatic design, is in how it is used.

Firearms owners are honest, decent citizens from all walks of life who use firearms safely and responsibly and believe in the right to choose for themselves whether to own a specific type of firearm.

Lawmakers concerned over illegal use of semi-automatic firearms or any type of firearm should concentrate their efforts on curbing criminal behavior, not penalizing or distrusting honest citizens who choose to own firearms. In the final analysis, it is the criminal alone who must be held accountable for violence.

The soundest, most effective means of deterring crime is the promise of swift, certain and severe punishment for criminal behavior.

Removing the criminal element from society through mandatory jail sentences works: no plea bargain, no probation, no parole.

Punishing criminals, not honest citizens, is the answer.

Illustration by Steve Kelley. Reprinted with permission.

Crime-Fighting Initiatives

The National Rifle Association (NRA) proposes a series of crime-fighting initiatives. The NRA will support these initiatives with the same vigor with which we oppose restrictive firearms laws.

● First, we propose the assignment of at least one Assistant U.S. Attorney in each district to prosecute felon-in-possession cases under 18 U.S.C. 922(g).

● Second, we propose a five-year freeze on plea bargain agreements when individuals are charged with violent or drug trafficking crimes.

● Third, we call for increased enforcement of the provisions of Public Law 99-308, the Firearms Owners' Protection Act. That law made it a federal felony, punishable with mandatory penalties, to use a firearm while committing a drug-trafficking offense. If the Justice Department finds that firearms were acquired from out-of-state in an investigation of gun-running rings, the federal government should step in.

● Fourth, we support the conversion to prisons of military bases scheduled to be closed, as well as reasonable funding mechanisms earmarked solely for the construction of Level III prison facilities.

● Fifth, we support the establishment of a special, expedited death penalty for those who kill police officers in the course of committing a felony.

● Sixth, we look forward to working with members of the Congress and the Administration to ensure that Section 6213 of Public Law 100-690 is carried out: That the Attorney General report to Congress this fall with a program allowing for the accurate and instantaneous screening of firearms purchasers at the point of purchase.

14   THE RISE IN URBAN VIOLENCE

GUN LAWS DO NOT ADDRESS THE UNDERLYING CAUSES OF VIOLENCE

Don B. Kates, Jr.

Don B. Kates, Jr. wrote the following reading in his capacity as a constitutional lawyer and criminologist. He wrote this article for the New York Times.

Points to Consider:

1. Have gun laws produced low rates of violence? Why or why not?

2. Explain how rates of violence vary with the relative size of a group.

3. Why do antigun advocates deny that violence is limited to a relatively small minority of deviates?

4. According to the author, how will violence be decreased?

Don B. Kates Jr., "Gun Bans Fail to Address Basic Causes of Violence in America," *Star Tribune*, February 7, 1989. Copyright © 1989 by The New York Times Company. Reprinted by permission.

Sadly, neither right- nor left-wing ideologists are willing to deal with the fact that reducing violence can not be achieved by easy, mechanistic solutions, such as banning guns.

Humane people react to the lack of ready solutions for tragedies like the Stockton, California, school massacre by crying out for gun control. I do not believe that gun bans can overcome the basic socioeconomic and cultural factors that produce violence.

Gun Laws and Crime Rates

Americans assume that such laws have produced Europe's low rates of violence. But studies find that these low rates long preceded gun bans. Indeed, such laws were pioneered, unsuccessfully, by high-crime American states in the late 19th and early 20th centuries, when most of Europe had no gun laws. It was only in the 1920s, when severe U.S. gun laws were generally being abandoned as unworkable, that Europe was adopting them.

Banning guns has not prevented modern Europe from suffering rates of political assassination and terrorism far exceeding those in the United States. Moreover, over the past 25 years even apolitical violence has risen more steeply in Europe than in America.

What's especially ironic is that Switzerland consistently has had low violence, political and apolitical. Yet any law-abiding Swiss may own guns, and every male of military age must keep at home an assault rifle more powerful than that used in the Stockton massacre.

Violence Rates Vary

The point is not that arming citizens will eliminate crime. What the European evidence shows is that crime can be at most marginally affected by gun policies. England's foremost gun-control analyst, Colin Greenwood, scoffs at claims that the availability of guns is a major cause of crime and that banning guns would reduce it.

ANOTHER VIEW ON GUN CONTROL

The tragic killing of five young schoolchildren in Stockton, California, has evoked the expected calls for more gun control. Yet gun control could impede the very social progress needed to stop such violent crime. . . .

Stricter gun control would do nothing to change any of the social conditions underlying such senseless violence. Poverty, oppression, and virulent ideologies like racism and militarism will last as long as capitalism does. Nor will gun control call into existence a comprehensive mental health system to help individuals before they crack.

"On Gun Control," The People, *February 11, 1989*

Claiming that in any society the number of guns will always suffice to arm the violent aberrant, Greenwood sees rates of violence as varying with the relative size of a group: Perhaps one in 300 Americans is violent, while the comparable figure for Japanese and Europeans may be one in 30,000.

Useless Situation?

Antigun advocates deny that violence is limited to a relatively small minority of deviates. They claim that murder is a crime primarily committed by good citizens who happen to have a loaded gun available in a moment of anger. But the uniform evidence from national and local homicide studies is that almost all murderers have serious crime histories.

Obviously such violent people should be disarmed—to the extent that laws can accomplish that. But guns already are outlawed to felons, juveniles and lunatics. Preventing good citizens who are not going to misuse guns from having them is worse than useless.

Reducing Violence

Sadly, neither right- nor left-wing ideologists are willing to deal with the fact that reducing violence cannot be achieved by easy, mechanistic solutions, such as banning guns.

Illustration by David Seavey. Copyright 1988, *USA Today*. Reprinted with permission.

Violence will be decreased only by painful, basic, long-term change in the socioeconomic and cultural factors that produce such a high number of violence-prone individuals in our society.

INTERPRETING EDITORIAL CARTOONS

This activity may be used as an individualized study guide for students in libraries and resource centers or as a discussion catalyst in small group and classroom discussions.

Although cartoons are usually humorous, the main intent of most political cartoonists is not to entertain. Cartoons express serious social comment about important issues. Using graphics and visual arts, the cartoonist expresses opinions and attitudes. By employing an entertaining and often light-hearted visual format, cartoonists may have as much or more impact on national and world issues as editorial and syndicated columnists.

Points to Consider:

1. Examine the cartoon in this activity. (See next page.)

2. How would you describe the message of this cartoon? Try to describe the message in one to three sentences.

3. Do you agree with the message expressed in this cartoon? Why or why not?

4. Are any of the readings in Chapter Two in basic agreement with this cartoon?

Cartoon by Pat Mitchell. Copyright 1984, *USA Today*. Reprinted with permission.

CHAPTER 3

RACIAL VIOLENCE: DEVASTATING OUR CITIES

THE BLACK UNDERCLASS: IDEAS IN CONFLICT

Morton M. Kondracke

Morton M. Kondracke wrote the following article in his capacity as a senior editor for The New Republic, *a weekly conservative journal.*

Points to Consider:

1. Describe the problems that plague the underclass.

2. How has the underclass developed?

3. What solutions are available to the black underclass?

4. Why is a spiritual renewal needed in black America?

Morton M. Kondracke, "The Two Black Americas," *The New Republic*, February 6, 1989, pp. 18-20. Reprinted by permission of *The New Republic,* © 1989, The New Republic, Inc.

The crisis of the underclass is so great that probably nothing short of a spiritual renewal in black America would really solve the problem.

The Black Underclass

Whatever troubles beset the black middle class, they are mild compared with those afflicting the underclass, which is relatively small, but by all indications is growing and deepening in its social pathology. It is hard to say how big it is, since statistical definitions of it are highly arbitrary. By one geographic definition, it's estimated that about 2.5 million people live in the most poverty-ridden census tracts of U.S. industrial cities. By one income definition, it's estimated that about four million blacks have lived for ten years below the poverty line. A slightly larger number, 4.3 million, lived in 1987 in families that could be termed "the poorest of the poor"—with an income below $4,528, half the poverty level. Either estimate could be low because of chronic undercounting of the poor, but either way, analysts put the size of the underclass at no more than 15 percent of the nation's 29 million blacks, and usually less. . . .

Besides abysmal education, illegitimacy, welfare-dependency, unemployment, bad housing, insufficient health care, and crime, the black underclass is being raked by drugs and AIDS, and an upsurge in child abuse connected to drug addiction. The director of one Boston-area settlement house says that the incidence of child sexual abuse in underclass families—black and white—is "nearly 100 percent." There was a 28 percent increase in the number of child abuse deaths reported between 1985 and 1986.

Development of the Underclass

How the underclass developed and what should be done about it are two of the most fiercely contested issues in social science and public policy. There are basically three schools of thought—the "welfare school: led by conservative Charles Murray of the Manhattan Institute, the "structural unemployment/social isolation" school led by black liberal Professor William Julius Wilson of the University of Chicago, and the "culture of poverty" school led by Professor Glenn Loury of Harvard, a black who is either a neoliberal or a conservative, depending on who's labeling him and the nuances of his most recent pronouncements.

ARE BLACK MALES AN ENDANGERED SPECIES?

The enormous dimensions of the problem are outlined in the Black Scholar *(June 1987) by black sociologist Robert Staples. . . .*

Staples cites the following statistics to support his grim assessment:

● *while black men comprise only 6 percent of the U.S. population, they make up half its male prisoners in local, state, and federal jails;*

● *more than 35 percent of all black men in U.S. cities are drug or alcohol abusers;*

● *more than 18 percent of black males drop out of high school;*

● *more than 50 percent of black men under the age of 21 are unemployed;*

● *46 percent of black men between the ages of 16 and 62 are not members of the labor force;*

● *approximately 32 percent of black men have incomes below the poverty level; and*

● *the homicide rate of black men is six times higher than for white men.*

Utne Reader, *Nov./Dec. 1988, p. 46*

A Conservative Approach

Murray, the darling of the Reagan right, argued in the 1984 book *Losing Ground* that liberal policies of the 1960s — notably increases in social spending, loosening of welfare regulations, Warren Court crime rulings, and the lowering of academic standards and discipline in public schools — encouraged young ghetto women to have babies, destroyed the work ethic, made crime pay, and made it harder for poor blacks to learn their way out of poverty. At the heart of Murray's argument was the observation that the percentage of black babies born to unmarried women began its steep climb in the mid-1960s, coinciding with the acceleration of social spending. In 1960, 22 percent of all black babies were born to unwed mothers; in 1970, the figure was 35 percent; in 1980, 55 percent. (For whites, the corresponding figures were two percent, six, and 11.)

Liberals claim that subsequent research, especially by Harvard's David Ellwood, has exploded Murray's thesis by demonstrating that illegitimacy continued to climb in the 1970s and 1980s even though welfare benefits failed to keep pace with inflation, and by showing that there is no state-by-state correlation between out-of-wedlock births and welfare levels. Murray now says what he really meant all along was that welfare, Medicaid, and other benefits enabled (rather than caused) ghetto girls to have children and no jobs and still get by, which they did.

A Liberal Opinion

Liberals prefer William Julius Wilson's thesis—advanced in the 1987 book *The Truly Disadvantaged*—that the deindustrialization of the American economy, which started in the early 1970s, and the movement of available jobs to suburbs left unskilled young ghetto males increasingly unemployable and undesirable as prospects for marriage. According to an earlier Wilson book, *The Declining Significance of Race*, the ability of stable, middle-class and working-class blacks to move out of the inner city left the ghettos increasingly occupied by the poor and the unemployed. So "the communities of the underclass are plagued by massive joblessness, flagrant and open lawlessness, and low-achieving schools . . . the residents of these areas, whether women and children of welfare families or aggressive street criminals, have become increasingly socially isolated from mainstream patterns of behavior."

Wilson's description of a self-perpetuating hell in the modern ghetto is not much different from that advanced by the "culture of poverty" school, but Loury thinks that both Wilson and Murray put too much emphasis on economic determinism and not enough on a breakdown of values in the ghetto and the failure of prominent blacks to help restore them. "Status is awarded for dope-dealing and for a woman to say, 'I'm a mother now,'" said Loury. "There are no centers of authority, public or private, saying, 'No, wait. What it means to be cool is not this.'". . .

Valid Explanations

Which of the three schools of thought has it right? Probably all of them, in some measure. Murray and Wilson seem to have valid explanations for the underclass culture that Loury laments: the perverse incentives of the welfare system and the desertion by more affluent blacks, conspired to help create the culture of poverty. It's certain, of course, that raw racism played a part, and it's likely that it continues to. Given the choice of hiring a

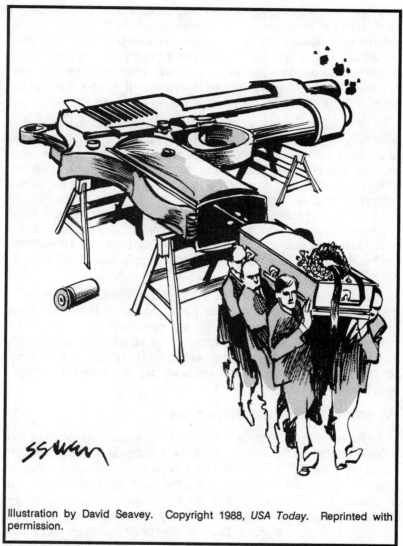

Illustration by David Seavey. Copyright 1988, *USA Today*. Reprinted with permission.

black male from the ghetto or somebody else, many white employers may well choose somebody else. The danger, as the culture of poverty deepens, is that this increasingly will be a sound economic decision on their part.

Solutions for the Black Underclass

So what's to be done about the black underclass? As a "thought experiment," Murray proposed in *Losing Ground* "scrapping the entire federal welfare and income-support structure for working-aged persons, including AFDC, Medicaid, food stamps, unemployment insurance, worker's compensation, subsidized housing, disability insurance, and the rest." He said, "It would leave the working-aged person with no recourse whatever except the job market, family members, friends, and public or private locally funded services. It is the Alexandrian solution: cut the knot, for there is no way to untie it."

Murray says he never really meant that, and knew it was politically unrealistic. His point, he says, is that no one knows how really to help the underclass and that federal efforts often end up doing more harm than good. Murray thinks that the continuing idleness among ghetto men during the economic recovery shows that lack of jobs is not their problem. "A different reality has been out there all along, it has been resolutely ignored, and it is finally beginning to intrude," Murray wrote last September in *Commentary*. "Liberals will increasingly be hearing themselves saying, 'Those people just don't want to work.'"

Murray thinks that drugs, AIDS, and crime are going to discourage even liberals from trying to solve the underclass problem, and make them settle for containment—establishing what he calls "custodial democracy" in which the poor simply will be provided with medical care, food, housing, and other social services "much as we currently do for American Indians who live on reservations."

Programs to Help the Underclass

If that's where things are heading, fortunately they have not arrived there yet. Liberals such as Wilson and Marian Wright Edelman [Children's Defense Fund president] still are proposing major programs to employ, educate, and otherwise help the underclass. Edelman's annual Children's Defense Budget contains programs in education, family planning, child care, job training, and employment to help the poor. Wilson says that increases in black male employment in Boston's tight labor market indicate that economic growth can help blacks, and he says that a new survey of 2,500 ghetto residents in Chicago indicates that they would work if they could find jobs, but are cut off from information about where the jobs are. "There is no absence of a work ethic," he said. He also cited a new University of Chicago study showing that a ghetto man who is employed is twice as likely to marry the mother of his children as one who is unemployed. Wilson doesn't deny that culture plays a role in keeping the underclass down, "but that's different from saying that these patterns are so deeply internalized that

100

they won't respond to changed circumstances."

Loury says he favors an amalgam of liberal and conservative ideas—plus increased efforts by black authority figures and ordinary middle-class blacks to work with ghetto youngsters and inculcate middle-class values. There is talk of an expanded Head Start program, of kindergarten beginning at age three, and of various other attempts to get young poor blacks out of the house as early and often as possible and into a more constructive environment.

Limited Resources

What George Bush can do will be limited by resources, and the crisis of the underclass is so great that probably nothing short of a spiritual renewal in black America would really solve the problem. (The Black Muslims, whatever else one thinks of them, do set crooked people straight. So does Alcoholics Anonymous.) Still, there are worthwhile public policy ideas around. Welfare re-reform is one, calling for a synthesis of left and right that would provide both the carrot and the stick: guaranteed jobs and day care along with the elimination of welfare. Opinion has moved in this general direction of late, but only slowly. The "workfare" bill passed by Congress last year barely qualified for the term. It requires work only if there is adequate state funding to provide guaranteed jobs and child care, and in most states there isn't. Someday, adequate funding will have to be provided. . . .

A Thousand Points of Light

Finally, there is Bush's "thousand points of light." With presidential leadership—starting with the Bush family and the White House staff—every business, church, civic group, social organization, government office, and country club in America could be encouraged to tutor kids, adopt schools, fund settlement houses, staff recreation centers, and otherwise rescue the rescuable. Bush could do for voluntary service what John F. Kennedy did for public service, though the effort has to be sustained, lest tutoring become the equivalent of 50-mile hikes, the short-lived fad of Kennedy's era. Bush claimed during the presidential campaign that he was "haunted by the lives lived by the children of our inner cities." He now has a chance to ease his pain. He should light a million points of light, and build to ten million.

16 RACIAL VIOLENCE: DEVASTATING OUR CITIES

SOCIAL PROGRAMS MUST BE RESTORED

Chris Booker

Chris Booker wrote this article as a special to the Guardian. *The* Guardian *describes itself as a weekly independent radical newspaper.*

Points to Consider:

1. What are the direct and indirect causes of the black under-class?

2. How have cuts in social programs affected the black community?

3. Why does drug dealing entice low-income people?

4. What measures must be taken to relieve the sense of hope-lessness within the low-income black community?

Chris Booker, "The Black 'Underclass'," *Guardian,* December 28, 1988, pp. 10-11.

The cause of this social crisis is the growing crack cocaine trade, as well as the prolonged free fall of basic living conditions within the low-income black community.

Increasingly desperate social and economic conditions in U.S. inner cities have spawned a new, more violent *lumpenproletariat* (or "underclass"), and triggered a national debate about how to respond to the crisis. . . .

The drug dealers are increasingly using automatic and semi-automatic weapons. Altogether, about 70 percent of Washington's slayings are believed to be drug-related and over 165 remain unsolved. During the four-year period from 1985 to 1988, 860 murders and 100,000 arrests took place. Most of these were drug-related.

The Cause of the Black Underclass

The direct cause of this social crisis in the "black underclass" is the growing crack cocaine trade which is accompanied by turf war that can only be settled by violence. More indirectly, the cause of the unraveling social fabric leading to this spasm of violence is the prolonged free fall of basic living conditions within the low-income black community. The signs of this ongoing crisis are everywhere; in the pervasiveness of homelessness, the overcrowded prison systems, the overburdened social service and charitable agencies, the malfunctioning educational system and in the demoralization and hopelessness experienced by a sizeable portion of low-income black youth.

The lack of faith on the part of many black youths in the opportunities for legitimate social mobility is at the core of the recent surge in drug dealing as a way of life. The heightened hurdles to prosperity raised by the social entrenchment of the Carter and Reagan eras has left the perception, to a large degree accurate, that illegal avenues to success offer the most realistic chance of coming to fruition.

Cuts in Social Programs

Soon after the Reagan administration took office in 1981, the merciless axe began to fall on those programs intended to raise the standard of living of working and low- and moderate-income people. Dramatic cuts in food stamps, Aid to Families with Dependent Children, federal job programs, child nutrition and

SOCIAL WELFARE PROGRAMS

To the extent that black people have made progress, we have to credit the civil rights revolution of the 1960s and the effects of the Great Society programs that are now out of fashion.

The laws, executive orders and judicial decisions of the 1960s empowered black people and removed many of the barriers in their way. Social welfare programs assisted many black people to get the incomes, health and nutrition care, and education they needed to enter the mainstream.

John E. Jacob (President and Chief Executive Officer of the National Urban League, Inc.), *"The Future of Black America,"* Vital Speeches of the Day, August 1, 1988

student aid, to name a few areas, reduced the prospects of social mobility almost instantly. Affirmative action programs, already under attack during the Carter years, began to wither on the vine.

Soon, the impact of these cuts on the black community were visible to any objective observer. The poverty rate for black women-headed families that included children under 18 rose from 56 percent in 1980 to 59 percent in 1985. For the nation's black community the impact was devastating. From 1978 through 1983, approximately 2.5 million black people were added to the ranks of the officially poor as the black poverty rate rose markedly from 30.6 percent in 1978 to 35.7 percent in 1983. Adding to this growing impoverishment was an acute crisis in affordable housing. The cessation of the construction for low-income housing, the tardy renovation and repair of existing housing projects combined with the forces of gentrification and traditional slumlord rent-gouging led to an enormous housing crisis for low-income blacks. The term "homelessness" entered the household vocabulary during the 1980s and nowhere was its impact felt so keenly as in the low-income black community.

Teen Pregnancy and the Black Community

The high rates of teen pregnancy in the 1980s within the black community, one indicator of the myopia of black youth trapped in the web of hopelessness, further aggravate the social and economic crisis within the community. Notwithstanding the contributions of the extended family which mitigates, to some extent, the lack of parenting skills possessed by teenagers, the high rates of teen pregnancy result in fewer resources of culture, education, wealth, and leadership in general that are available to aid the development of youth.

Further, the increase in teen pregnancy is an important contributor to the trend of families headed by single women. Economist Julianne Malveaux recently wrote that within the service sector "black women are overrepresented by a factor of three of four as chambermaids, welfare service aides, cleaners and nurse's aides." She notes that, significantly, 64 percent of black women employed in service jobs are paid at full-time rates of less than poverty wages.

This fact takes on added significance when the stagnation of the minimum wage is considered. Presently, 741,000 blacks earn a minimum wage that has not increased since 1981 when it rose to $3.35, the result of legislation passed in 1977. Today, the minimum wage is only worth $2.68 in 1981 dollars. With a poverty line set at $7,230 in 1984 for a two-person family, a full-time worker at the minimum wage would earn only $6,986 working every week of the year without a vacation. This decline in the purchasing power of the minimum wage impairs the ability of young people to establish independent households and stabilize families.

Drugs and Money

The prospect of big earnings by drug dealing enters into this social context of scarcity, bringing with it the chance to enjoy the consumer goods other sectors of U.S. society take for granted. A recent study by the Greater Washington Research Center estimates that by their 30th birthday approximately 20 percent of low-income D.C. males have been charged with drug dealing. Crack dealers often earn over $2,000 per day. The deterrent of imprisonment has faded as the jails become too crowded to house youths for long periods of time. Since other family members also enjoy the benefits of prosperity they sometimes become involved with the enterprise. Doris Wilder, a Detroit drug counselor, said, "We've had situations where a grandmother was using and selling crack as well as most of her children and grandchildren."

The total of these various indices of misery add up to much more than the sum of the parts. It is not surprising that black college attendance has plummeted. While in 1977 about the

Illustration by Eleanor Mill.

same proportion of blacks as whites who graduated from high school went to college, by 1983 the rate for blacks had dropped to 39 percent while the rate for whites rose to 55 percent.

Beginnings and Solutions

Surrounding the debate concerning solutions to the problem of the "black underclass" are the issues related to its genesis. The term, increasingly in vogue, has come to connote a permanently impoverished and crime-ridden sector of black society for whom, say some conservative ideologists, further government programs will do little. Indeed, they contend these well-intentioned programs did more to harm this segment of society than they did to help. . . .

Conservative efforts, similarly, offer slim hope that any sizeable portion of a generation of "underclass" youth will be positively touched. These include proposals for independent business ownership, a subminimum wage for youth (black youth in actuality) and tenant ownership of public housing. The latter proposal, comprising almost the whole program of the conservative right for the alleviation of conditions facing the low-income black community, is offered almost as a panacea. The Kenilworth-Parkside apartments have been showcased for almost four years by conservatives. Yet, it is little substitute for specific measures to tackle the serious problems of this community.

Several questions remain to be answered. How can a housing project provide the employment needed by a community with a chronic unemployment problem? How can tenants afford to maintain these houses over the years? How does this meet the other needs that only government can provide on a large scale?

Admirable efforts by local coalitions, community organizations and religious institutions to meet human needs in housing, hunger and other areas fall far short of satisfying the growing need in these areas.

Economic and Social Justice

Liberal analyst Douglas Glasgow places great emphasis on overcoming unemployment. "No new actions are more critical to reversing the underclass condition than putting the ideal labor force to work and providing livable incomes," he notes. "Economic justice demands, at minimum, that blacks equally share the benefits of prosperity and the hardships of recessions on par with all other Americans. A sensitive strategy—affirmative action—provides a tested model to undergird efforts to achieve this goal," Glasgow says.

There are several measures that must be taken immediately to relieve the sense of hopelessness felt by many within the low-income black community. In the short term, restoring some of the programs slashed early in the Reagan administration would begin to slow down the rate of decline. A renewed emphasis on job training, child nutrition, pre-natal care, drug treatment and affordable housing programs is clearly demanded by the seriousness of the present social and economic crisis of the community.

In the longer term, measures that have long been proposed by the left are necessary to begin to realize the lofty goals of equal opportunity and social justice. Guarantees of decent employment, education, medical care and affordable housing are suitable long-term goals. However, the key ingredient to their attainment is the political mobilization of the low-income black community itself. It is doubtful that conservative or liberal forces will contribute to this: indeed, this is their worst nightmare. Clearly, whether this mass mobilization will come about depends upon the decisions of the left, especially the black left, regarding which areas are accorded priority in its strategies for the future.

17 RACIAL VIOLENCE: DEVASTATING OUR CITIES

POOR BLACKS MUST RELY ON THEMSELVES

Walter Williams

Walter Williams is a syndicated columnist. His article originally appeared in the Conservative Chronicle.

Points to Consider:

1. What are the chances that a young black man will be murdered?

2. How many black murder victims die at the hands of other blacks?

3. Why does the author believe civil rights activists "have it backwards"?

4. Describe why black self-help organizations are offering hope.

Walter Williams, "Black Victims," *Conservative Chronicle*, p. 16. Reprinted with permission from Heritage Features Syndicate.

There are black ministers and community activists demanding that people take responsibility for their own lives.

Many blacks live under conditions most Americans would consider outrageous. Public safety, considered the norm in most places, is rare in inner-city ghettos.

Blacks and Murder

According to the National Center for Health Statistics, the murder rate among blacks is 34 per 100,000 of the population compared to 7 per 100,000 for whites. Young black men stand a one in 21 chance of being murdered, making murder the leading cause of death among young black men. In statistics cited by Jay Parker, editor of the *Lincoln Review,* 6,833 black males were murdered in 1983 alone; this is nearly as many as were killed during the entire Vietnam War. Just about all (95 percent) of black murder victims dies at the hands of other blacks.

Many murders are a result of gang wars, which often occur in and around school premises. Victims and perpetrators are as young as 11 years old. Sometimes a person is murdered for something as trivial as arguments over designer shirts or being in the "wrong" neighborhood.

Upsurge in Racial Incidents

Over the past several years, we've seen an upsurge in racial incidents like the Howard Beach, N.Y., affair which resulted in the death of a black teenager. Benjamin Hooks, executive director of the NAACP, tells us the Reagan administration is responsible for the resurgence of racism. The Chicago Defender's Leroy Thomas said, "People seem to think it's open season on blacks." Georgia State Sen. Julian Bond and other civil rights activists echo similar sentiments.

Racial incidents should be deplored and prevented. But civil rights activists have it backwards. Yes, it's open season on blacks, but it's not whites doing the killing. Blacks would be infinitely better off if they only had to live in fear of being murdered by whites. Fearing whites only, blacks could fearlessly walk their neighborhoods at night; they wouldn't have to worry about their daughters, wives, and mothers being raped; and they could conduct their businesses without the constant fear of robbery, burglary, and assault.

BEYOND GOVERNMENT

If we attribute minority failure solely to racism we misdefine the problem and look in the wrong direction for the solutions. Like the man who looks for his keys under the lamp post, even though he lost them in the dark, we shall search for the wrong solutions.

As Glenn C. Loury, a black author, put it:

"It is now beyond dispute that many of the problems of contemporary black American life lie outside the reach of effective government action, and require for their successful resolution actions that can only be undertaken by the black community itself. These problems involve at their core the values, attitudes, and behaviors of individual blacks."

Richard D. Lamm, former Governor of Colorado, in a speech before the Denver Rotary Club, January 26, 1989

When black civil rights activists, ministers, and politicians speak in pious condemnation of the relatively few instances where a white murders a black, and cry about civil rights violation, do they think those 6,000-plus blacks murdered in 1983 did not have their civil rights violated? Or do they think dying at the hands of a fellow black is somehow more pleasing to the victim?

Black-on-Black Crime

If we were to question black-on-black crime, we'd be told that racial discrimination and poverty are the root causes, after first being denounced as racists. If racism and poverty is the cause, why was the murder rate among blacks lower during earlier periods when there was much more racism and poverty? Keeping a keen eye on blacks murdered by whites, and dismissing blacks murdered by blacks as caused by racism and poverty, is to condemn 7,000 blacks to death each year.

Glimmer of Hope

Despite this gloomy state of affairs, there's a glimmer of hope on the horizon. There's a growing number of black self-help organizations. Black organizations, like the Washington-based Center for Neighborhood Enterprises and the Institute for

111

Illustration by Locher. Reprinted by permission: Tribune Media Services.

Independent Education, are expanding their roles. Moreover, there are black ministers and community activists, four of whom were featured on a recent *Oprah Winfrey Show*, involved in resurrecting black institutions, helping—and demanding—that people take responsibility for their own lives. These voices are being heard with increasing frequency. Thank God. Decent Americans, irrespective of color, should roll up their sleeves and give them encouragement.

18 RACIAL VIOLENCE: DEVASTATING OUR CITIES

SEXISM KNOCKS BLACK MEN DOWN

Jack Kammer

Jack Kammer is a free-lance writer specializing in gender-related social problems. He wrote this article for the Baltimore Sun.

Points to Consider:

1. How does our society view men? How does our society view women?

2. In what way does sexism affect the young black male?

3. Why does the author disagree with Jesse Jackson's statement regarding how much money women earn?

4. What happened during Oprah Winfrey's interview with Fred Hayward?

Jack Kammer, "Sexism Knocks Black Men Down," *Star Tribune,* April 4, 1989. Reprinted by permission of *The Baltimore Evening Sun.*

113

Racism knocks black men down. Sexism, plodding heavily on the premise that the value of men is equal to the money they make, then comes along to kick them.

The Soothing Sham

The most apparent fact about the current plague of drug-related murders wracking America's inner cities is that the vast majority of the people involved are black. Since most of us are oblivious to the gender-based problems of men and boys, we attach no significance to the fact that they are also male.

If hundreds of black women were slaughtering each other in a mad attempt to earn illicit money, policy makers most certainly would inquire into the gender basis of their turmoil. We are accustomed to thinking of women as victims.

But we live in a society that can stare directly at desperate, defiant men and fail to see beyond the soothing sham that "it's a man's world."

Gender Problems

We are blind to the fact that being male can be a problem, especially for poor blacks. We cannot fathom the frustration of being a man with nothing in a society that tells men they have it all — or are not worth anything at all. In a recent song that hit the top of the black-music charts, a woman cooed, "You gotta have a J.O.B. if you wanna be with me."

But make no mistake. The problem of evaluating men solely on their ability to perform economically is not confined to the black community, nor even to the United States. In Germany, for instance, the same sexist tune is sung with different lyrics: "Women are what they are. Men are what they do."

In other words, women are valuable merely by virtue of their existence as women. Men are worthless without performance.

Sexism and Black Men

Denied, as they are, the reasonable expectation of success, young black men are especially vulnerable to this form of sexism. Without money, they are consigned to the living hell of feeling inferior to and unworthy of their female counterparts.

In anguished, pathetic, violent and illegal ways, they try to compensate. They have nothing; therefore they are nothing. What can they lose?

┌───┐
│   │
│   **MURDER VICTIMS**   │
│   │
│   *In the U.S., a white male has a 1-in-186 chance of*│
│   *becoming a murder victim. For black men, the odds are*│
│   *one in 29. And for those living in Washington, D.C., the*│
│   *South Bronx or Chicago's South Side, the murder rate odds*│
│   *for black males soar to less than one out of 20.* │
│   │
│   *Manning Marable, "Community Organizing Combats Crime," Guardian,*│
│   *March 8, 1989*   │
│   │
└───┘

We cause our cities to decay from their cores when we tell our young urban men that intrinsically they have no value. We rob black men of their determination and resiliency when we make them feel essentially worthless; we only hope they seek and find productive work as a salve for their psychic wound. We delude ourselves when we think that minimum-wage jobs will provide young men with the self-esteem they need to thrive in a world in which men, especially black men, are expendable.

Men and Money

The problem is not primarily a lack of money. The problem is that contemporary society focuses too much on the connection between men and money.

We would do better to affirm to ourselves and to our young men their inherent value as people—every bit as good and noble as women regardless of how much they make—and then to encourage them to build on that foundation of strength and self-esteem. A solid self-image will not disappear as fast as a job might.

Black Society Has Been Unkind

The cruelties perpetrated upon black men by white society hardly need to be recounted. But black society, too, has been unkind. . . .

In his stump speech during the 1988 presidential campaign, Jesse Jackson railed against the fact that women earn less than men. He pointed out the injustice of the pay differential by saying, "But women can't buy bread for less than men can. They can't buy milk and eggs for less than men can."

True enough, but regardless of their income, women can gain access to other invaluable commodities—the love of children, for instance, and the interest of the opposite sex. But men, as we have seen, are generally rewarded with these things in direct proportion to their income.

A Revealing Interview

Before she moved to Chicago and national prominence, Oprah Winfrey was the co-host of a Baltimore talk show. On one program she unwittingly helped prove with crystal clarity that there is such a thing as sexism against men—and that it bears down especially hard on black men.

During an interview with Fred Hayward, director of Men's Rights, Inc., an organization concerned with sexism and men's problems, she tried to induce her guest to concede that though men's issues might make interesting conversation, they are insignificant compared to women's issues. Hayward, one of the nation's most insightful commentators on gender problems facing men, was not about to concede any such thing.

Winfrey pressed. "Oprah," Hayward responded, "proportional to the population, there are eight times as many blacks in jail as whites. What does that tell you?"

Winfrey said that told her that blacks live under more social and economic pressure than whites. Hayward agreed wholeheartedly, then made his case: "Oprah, proportional to the population, there are 24 times as many men in jail as women. What does that tell you?"

Perhaps it is not merely by coincidence that Winfrey co-produced and starred in the television mini-series "The Women of Brewster Place," a story that so achingly empathized with black women and gave black men such short shrift.

Racism and Sexism

How many black men, we should ask as we ponder the escalating whirlwind of urban crime, are in jail? How many black men risk everything for the self-esteem drug money can buy?

We should pay attention not only to society's different treatment of blacks and whites, but also and especially to our different treatment of black men and black women.

Racism knocks black men down. Sexism, plodding heavily on the premise that the value of men is equal to the money they make, then comes along to kick them.

Illustration by Craig MacIntosh. Reprinted by permission of *Star Tribune, Newspaper of the Twin Cities.*

WHAT IS RACE BIAS?

This activity may be used as an individualized study guide for students in libraries and resource centers or as a discussion catalyst in small group and classroom discussions.

The capacity to recognize an author's point of view is an essential reading skill. The skill to read with insight and understanding involves the ability to detect different kinds of opinions or bias. Sex bias, race bias, ethnocentric bias, political bias, and religious bias are five basic kinds of opinions expressed in editorials and all literature that attempts to persuade. They are briefly defined below.

Five Kinds of Editorial Opinions or Bias

SEX BIAS—The expression of dislike for and/or feeling of superiority over the opposite sex or a particular sexual minority

RACE BIAS—The expression of dislike for and/or feeling of superiority over a racial group

ETHNOCENTRIC BIAS—The expression of a belief that one's own group, race, religion, culture, or nation is superior. Ethnocentric persons judge others by their own standards and values.

POLITICAL BIAS—The expression of political opinions and attitudes about domestic or foreign affairs

RELIGIOUS BIAS—The expression of a religious belief or attitude

---

Guidelines

Read through the following statements and decide which ones represent race opinion or bias. Evaluate each statement by using the method indicated below.

- **Mark (R) for statements that reflect any race opinion or bias.**
- **Mark (F) for any factual statements.**
- **Mark (O) for statements of opinion that reflect other kinds of opinion or bias.**
- **Mark (N) for any statements that you are not sure about.**

1. The homicide rate of black men is six times higher than for white men.

2. Given the choice of hiring a black male from the ghetto or somebody else, many white employers may well choose somebody else.

3. Probably nothing short of a spiritual renewal in black America would really solve the problems of the underclass.

4. The direct cause of the social crisis in the black underclass is the growing crack cocaine trade and the violence that is usually associated with it.

5. The high rates of teen pregnancy within the black community further aggravate the social and economic crisis within the community.

6. Black Americans are more socially, politically, and economically disenfranchised than they have been for more than a century.

7. Many blacks live under conditions most Americans would consider outrageous.

8. There are black ministers and community activists demanding that people take responsibility for their own lives.

9. Over the past several years, there has been an upsurge in racial incidents.

10. Racism knocks black men down.

11. Young black men are vulnerable to certain forms of sexism.

12. We should pay attention to our different treatment of black men and black women.

CHAPTER 4

DEALING WITH URBAN VIOLENCE

POVERTY CAUSES INNER-CITY VIOLENCE

Tristram Coffin

Tristram Coffin is the editor of The Washington Spectator, *a semimonthly publication of the Public Concern Foundation.*

Points to Consider:

1. What are the four factors that contribute to violence?

2. How has poverty in inner-city slums changed in the past 20 years?

3. Why did the students at Howard University protest the election of Lee Atwater to Howard's board of trustees?

4. Describe the connection between drugs and violence.

Tristram Coffin, ed., "Violent Crime: Cause and Cure," *The Washington Spectator,* May 15, 1989, pp. 1-2.

We must change the social and economic reasons for the epidemic of violence and get rid of guns and drugs.

"With terrifying frequency and no respite apparent, the gunfire continues to ring out this week with the bloodiest single day Washington can remember." (*Washington Post* editorial)

Homicides take the lives of more children in the District of Columbia than any other single type of injury, including car accident, house fire, or drowning. This is not an exclusive phenomenon of Washington. The overcrowded slums of other big American cities, such as New York, Miami and Los Angeles, are ridden with senseless violent crime. It is a form of incoherent, unplanned rebellion against a society which, the young complain, deprives them of the good life they see on TV. It is also a symptom of what Noam Chomsky says is the mass alienation of Americans.

Four Factors

The violence springs from four factors:

● The sullen rage of mostly boys and young men who live in poverty and squalor and are taunted by visions of affluence and ease which they have no hope of reaching. They are in part victims of the stress on materialism and self-interest of the Reagan era.

The young understand the spur that goads them. They spoke their minds at a meeting in a Washington high school called to discuss the crime crisis. Some comments: "We have to show there's more to life than shooting or stabbing someone, or wearing clothes that cost a fortune. . . .Our biggest problem is that teen-agers in this city have low self-esteem. If you don't respect yourself, how can you respect other people?"

● The easy access to guns, which become the substitute for fists, the usual weapon of the young. Murder is so common in the ghettoes that the social horror has been lost. A mother who has kept her son from Jordan High School in the Watts area of Los Angeles explains, "I don't want my son killed up there. It's as simple as that."

● The desperate craving for drugs to relieve boredom, melancholy, self-doubt, and want.

● Gang warfare built around profits from crack, a derivative of cocaine.

THE LEADING KILLER

Violence has replaced infection as the leading killer of young people in the United States, a University of Minnesota researcher reported in the latest issue of the Journal of the American Medical Association.

Accidents, homicide and suicide, the three leading causes of violent death in the young, account for more than 77 percent of death in the 15- to 24-year-old group, according to Dr. Robert Blum, head of the university's adolescent health program.

Gordon Slovut, *"'U' Researcher Says Violence Has Replaced Infection as Leading Killer of Young in U.S.,"* Star Tribune, *July 26, 1987*

Social Reasons Listed

The cure is not only to build more prisons, for they have become too often graduate schools of crime. Rather, we must change the social and economic reasons for the epidemic of violence and get rid of guns and drugs.

First, a look at the young fellow who wantonly shoots to kill or wound, and the environment in which he lives.

● He is male, in his teens or 20s. The early years of his life, a time when character is formed, were spent in poverty. The Children's Defense Fund points out, "our children are growing poorer and poorer while our nation is growing richer." (Average income of the lowest fifth of all persons in the U.S. dropped nearly 11 percent from 1973 to 1987, while average income for the highest fifth rose 24 percent, according to a House Ways and Means Committee study.) Within a few years, suggests the National Education Association, 40 percent of all secondary students will come from families living in poverty. This is due in part to the high birth rate among the poor.

The National League of Cities finds that poverty in inner-city slums has become more persistent and concentrated over the last 20 years, and its victims have less chance of escape. The *Philadelphia Inquirer* reports that families living in inner-city poverty areas nearly doubled between 1980 and 1985, from 884,000 to 1.7 million households.

● He is of a minority, black or Hispanic, and has felt the sting of rebuff. As a child he had little of the tender, loving care that

123

a close-knit family can offer. His father was nowhere to be seen. His mother was so intent on finding the bare necessities that she had little time for him. His schooling was superficial. His moral values came largely from the street and TV.

Poverty the Norm

National Education Association president Mary H. Putrell says, "We are finding that poverty and lack of parental support, money, and language are the norm rather than the exception." From 1974 to 1983, more than 21 percent of blacks in big cities were poor; among non-blacks, less then 3 percent.

A teacher tells the *Washington Post* that she has been "moved by children who fill up on water or steal sandwiches out of their friends' lunch boxes because they are hungry, or fall asleep in class because they do not have the proper nutrition."

The Children's Defense Fund states: "It is the lack of loving care that turns children into savage teen-agers and adults. . . The number of youths held for alcohol and drug offenses increased by 56 percent between 1985 and 1987. . . . The rage and pain of these homeless, hopeless, abused, alienated children will continue to explode in our faces."

Their health has deteriorated. "When the savings and loan industry has a crisis, political leaders find at least $60 billion to bail them out. When our children are dying and being disabled from preventable causes, our political leaders. . . .say we cannot afford the few billions to build a health floor."

The *New York Times* describes a lodging for the poor in Washington: "Scarred and unkempt, the motel is now shelter for 200 adults and 700 children. One family to a room, month after overcrowded month, even for years. . . .Teachers from the elementary school frequently come in search of absent pupils, often finding that the children are embarrassed by their clothing and status in life."

The *Los Angeles Times* describes a lodging there: "Torn blankets, piles of rags, old clothes, dirty pillows, a few scattered utensils or cups — the detritus of a privileged city in which pauperized men and women try to create a normal life." (President Reagan and Congress cut housing finds by more than 70 percent during his eight years. His last budget had no new funds for public housing, and Bush did not ask for any in his budget message.)

"Quitting," Rebellion, and Violence

What about the kids when they grow into adolescence? The

E. Gentry for The People

Illustration by Ed Gentry. Reprinted with permission of *The People.*

story is told of a black mother in Washington, proud of her son who won excellent grades in high school and was determined to make his way up. Six months after graduation and a diligent search for a job, he was still idle. She was afraid he would "quit" his resolve and sink back into the hopelessness that held so many of his peers.

The *Los Angeles Times* tells of two such men: Wilson and Butler now walk the tough streets of Skid Row wondering what to do. They pass by thousands who have 'quit,' people not much different from themselves. 'Quitting' offers relief from the constant struggle for housing and employment, but often it means battling with nightmares of crime, crack, cocaine and alienation."

The rebellion too often veers into violence. This is not true of those from families that are more stable, economically and socially. This was reflected in the student uprising at Howard University, America's leading black college. The *Washington Post* reported: "In one of the largest demonstrations at Howard University in recent years, students disrupted the convocation ceremonies to protest the election of Lee Atwater, chairman of the Republican National Committee, to Howard's board of trustees." They occupied the Administration building. Police battered the doors and a leader shouted, "We've got to remember Dr. King. He's looking down on us. So don't be violent. Everybody, hands in pockets, and don't move whatever they do."

Atwater was a symbol to the black students of that part of American society which they trust the least — white, wealthy, privileged people who run the show.

Drugs and Violence

Drugs are a prelude to much of the violent crime. After a bloody night in Washington when four were killed and five wounded by gunfire, the *Washington Post* reported: "Police said most of the slayings have been drug-related killings that involve territorial disputes, buyers and sellers who are fighting, persons acting under the influence of drugs or thieves seeking money to buy drugs."

The use of crack is concentrated among the urban poor, while drug use in more well-to-do communities has decreased, according to recent studies. Crack is cheap, as little as $5 a "rock," and it offers a momentary escape from the degrading life of the ghetto. Yet, as Barbara Ehrenreich writes in *Ms.*: "Drug frenzy is not. . . .a quick and harmless high. It is an obsession, overshadowing all other concerns, and capable of leaving a society drained, impotent and brain-damaged."

A New York drug enforcement agent says, "I can tell you that crack is clearly the most pernicious drug we've ever seen." A Miami homicide detective calls it "the worst drug ever," with users "terribly addicted. Young people are willing to kill for it."

So overwhelming is the use of crack that treatment centers cannot care for the torrent of addicts, who tend to be young and poor.

126

20   DEALING WITH URBAN VIOLENCE

CRIME CAUSES INNER-CITY POVERTY

James K. Stewart

James K. Stewart wrote this article in his capacity as director of the National Institute of Justice. He was formerly commander of criminal investigations in the Oakland Police Department and a White House Fellow.

Points to Consider:

1. Describe the ways in which crime affects the poor.

2. How does crime affect inner-city housing and property values?

3. Why do criminals tyrannize poor neighbors?

4. What is the best anti-poverty policy?

"The Urban Strangler: How Crime Causes Poverty in the Inner City" by James K. Stewart is reprinted (excerpted) from the Summer 1986 issue of *Policy Review,* the quarterly publication of The Heritage Foundation, 214 Massachusetts Ave., N.E., Washington, D. C. 20002.

America is beginning to take the steps necessary to fight terrorism overseas; the time has come to fight the even more threatening terrorism in our own cities.

The idea that poverty causes crime goes back at least as far as Aristotle, who called poverty "the parent of revolution and crime." But in the American inner city, the relationship is exactly the reverse. Poverty doesn't cause crime. Crime causes poverty—or more precisely, crime makes it harder to break out of poverty. The vast majority of poor people are honest, law-abiding citizens whose opportunities for advancement are stunted by the drug dealers, muggers, thieves, rapists, and murderers who terrorize their neighborhoods. These predators are not Robin Hoods of some 1960s ideal; they are career criminals who are destroying the labor and hopes of the poor and they are as oppressive as the most avaricious totalitarian regime.

Stealing from the Poor

The most obvious way that criminals prey upon the poor is by robbing them of their property—and sometimes their lives. According to the Bureau of Justice Statistics, 9.6 percent of households with incomes of less than $7,500 were burglarized in 1984. This was the highest victimization rate in the country, nearly twice as high as for households in the $25,000 to $30,000 range, and the poorest also suffer the highest victimization rates for violent crimes. Households with incomes in the $7,500 to $14,999 range suffer the highest median economic losses from personal crimes, including robbery, assault, and theft. Since poor people often cannot afford insurance, and since personal property accounts for almost all of their capital, the theft of a TV, furniture, or car can be devastating. Robberies of cash or checks—for rent, welfare, or Social Security—may at one stroke eliminate a family's ability to pay for home, food, or future.

The typical criminal does not rob from the rich to aid the poor; he steals from the helpless to help himself. There's a routine on "Mother's Day"—the day every week when welfare checks arrive in the mail—of criminals extorting or stealing checks from welfare recipients or looting them from their mailboxes. Automatic deposits or safe deposit boxes aren't necessarily safer, since a criminal who knows your weekly income can collect on penalty of physical assault.

CRACKDOWN ON GANGS

Police arrested more than 1,000 people in a weekend blitz against drug dealers and street gangs responsible for violence that has killed hundreds a year.

"L.A. Police Arrest 1,000 in Crackdown on Gangs," Star Tribune, *April 11, 1988*

The Costs of Crime

The less direct costs of crime to the poor may be even more destructive. The traditional means by which poor people have advanced themselves — overtime, moonlighting, or education to improve future opportunities — can easily be obstructed by crime and fear. Why risk a late job or night school if the return home means waiting at deserted bus stops and walking past crowds of threatening teenagers? A secretary declines overtime opportunities if they extend into the evening because she fears being robbed between the taxi and her front door. A husband gives up night school rather than leave his wife and young children alone at home.

Crime and Property Values

Crime lowers property values in inner cities, making it harder for poor people to accumulate capital and borrow money. Studies in Chicago by Mario Rizzo and Barton A. Smith have shown that for every rise of one percent in the crime rate, rents and home values drop to 0.2 to 0.3 percent. The result is disastrous for families saving and scrimping to build up some modest capital; only by moving can they improve their lot.

Renters, of course, may benefit from the decline in property values, but their gain is only temporary. If landlords have no incentive to keep up maintenance on their properties, both the quality and quantity of housing stock will deteriorate and renters will lose in the end. The vast stretches of vacant buildings in the South Bronx are probably due as much to crime as to rent control; even if landlords could raise the rents, no one who could afford the increases would want to live there.

Similarly, crime can destroy even the most attractive public housing projects, turning them into catastrophes for their tenants. With their long hallways, lonely elevators and stairwells, and absence of street life, public housing high-rises trap and

129

deliver victims to their criminal predators; often they are more treacherous breeding grounds of crime than the squalid tenements they replaced. It was largely because of crime that the Pruitt-Igoe housing complex in St. Louis became uninhabitable and had to be demolished. The Cabrini-Green apartments in Chicago remain in use, but they are ridden with fear.

Crime and Business

Crime strangles commerce and industry in the inner city, and therefore makes it harder for poor people to get jobs. Wherever people are afraid, the market cannot be free. And the high crime rates of poor neighborhoods prevent their residents from taking full advantage of the employment opportunities offered by America's market economy. . . .

Perhaps the most serious threat to business is that customers and suppliers are scared away. The Chicago study noted that "more than half of the businessmen in both neighborhoods reported that some or all of their suppliers had complained of feeling unsafe in the area.". . .

Criminal Recycling Centers

Criminals can tyrannize poor neighborhoods because they are not significantly threatened by the criminal justice system. Only 20 percent of reported crimes are ever solved. And a large proportion of crimes—especially in poor neighborhoods—are never reported. Among households with incomes of less than $7,500, only 40 percent of burglaries and fewer than one-third of all household crimes are ever reported. In poor neighborhoods, people are usually reluctant to turn someone in, call the police, or testify in court. Their reticence is understandable, for local justice policy quickly releases criminal suspects and then delays their trials for months. Victims and key witnesses are therefore exposed to opportunities for intimidation by criminals or their confederates. . . .

Eradicating the Parasite

The best anti-poverty policy is a vigorous attack on crime in poor communities. Yellow fever was finally cured when attention was shifted from treating the dying patients to controlling the mosquito that carried the disease. Likewise, inner cities can be restored to economic health if we eradicate the parasite that infects them—crime. . . .

In Oakland, a security program was initiated in 1982 by a

Cartoon by Stein. © by *National Review,* Inc., 150 East 35 Street, New York, NY 10016. Reprinted with permission.

group of private developers. Clorox and IBM are among the major tenants of Bramalea Corporation properties who contribute about $300,000 annually to provide for a police enhancement program of the 40-block downtown business district. The program increased the police foot patrol in the area and added a mounted patrol, as well as more motorbike and motorscooter patrols—which create a greater sense of protection and accessibility to police than car patrol. The program also made a well publicized effort to curtail incivilities and disorderly behavior in the neighborhood.

Property crimes, which dropped nine percent citywide from 1982 to 1983, fell by 20 percent in this central area. Declines in strongarm robbery, purse snatchings, commercial burglary, and auto theft were particularly dramatic. But more important than the drop in crime was the greater sense of security and confidence people felt, indicated by the larger flow of orderly pedestrian traffic. One local businessman commented, "I don't hear about muggings any more." A bank manager noted that use of the bank's cafeteria dropped significantly (suggesting more workers were going out to eat in the neighborhood), and merchants reported greater lunchtime shopping by employees.

The improved security has been decisive in attracting and

131

retaining businesses. IBM came into the neighborhood on the basis of the security program. One business owner noted, "If we didn't have the foot patrol and increased police presence downtown, I wouldn't be in business in Oakland."

A project in Portland, Oregon, to improve the security of the Union Avenue commercial strip also led to a significant reduction in commercial burglary, following improvements in street lighting and store security. Reversing a period of decline, businessmen reported that gross sales were holding steady or even increasing since the lighting and security changes.

Improved security is also the key to a remarkably successful urban project in Watts. The riots that destroyed parts of the Los Angeles community 20 years ago wiped out marginal businesses and appeared to have killed off new business growth. New enterprises could not take root because crime made people unwilling to work, shop, or make deliveries in the area. Investors wouldn't touch the neighborhood, even with the prospect of capturing the market, because of the low customer traffic and risks of high losses.

The first commercial enterprise of any kind to be built since the riots was the Martin Luther King, Jr. Shopping Center, which opened in 1984 at a location formerly called "Charcoal Alley" as a result of its fiery devastation in the riots. Estimated first year sales were about $45 million, or about $350 per leasable square foot—more than three times the average revenues of first-year shopping centers. Though it was built in one of the most violent and crime-ridden areas of the city, no major acts of violence or vandalism have occurred there. "The success of the shopping center shows that you can make money and create jobs here without fear of the stereotype that says you can't do business in the ghetto because of crime," said Dr. Clyde Oden, a Watts physician who is president of the Watts Health Foundation. . . .

Real Social Security

The programs in Brooklyn, Oakland, Portland, and Watts show that, if security is provided, business can take root in even the most hostile environment. Reducing crime and its disruptive effect on community ties eliminates the largest and most devastating obstacle to development in many poor neighborhoods. And where businesses can develop, they encourage further growth and help create a community's cohesiveness and identity.

Crime is a hazard to everyone in our society, but it hurts the poor the most; the wealthy and the middle class can call upon private and community resources to cushion them from some of its dangers. The first step in any urban anti-poverty program must therefore begin with the reduction of crime. This means more vigorous prosection of predatory criminals and more vigorous protection of people in poor neighborhoods. America is beginning to take the steps necessary to fight terrorism overseas; the time has come to fight the even more threatening terrorism in our own cities.

21   DEALING WITH URBAN VIOLENCE

GETTING TOUGH WITH DELINQUENTS MAY NOT HELP

National Council on Crime and Delinquency

Established in 1907 by professionals in the criminal and juvenile justice field, the National Council on Crime and Delinquency (NCCD) works to control crime through improving the criminal justice system. It promotes programs and policies that are fair, humane, and economically sound. Its major fields of effort are in research, standard setting, education, training, surveys, technical information gathering and dissemination. It operates the largest citizen action program of its kind in the country.

This reading is excerpted from an NCCD report on violent juvenile crime.

Points to Consider:

1. Describe the rates of violent youth crime.

2. What happened to delinquents after they were released from incarceration?

3. How would an increase in incarceration of juvenile offenders affect the crime rate?

4. Summarize the various ways to deal with violent juveniles.

National Council on Crime and Delinquency, *Facts about Violent Juvenile Crime*, May 1988. Reprinted with permission of the National Council on Crime and Delinquency.

The bulk of the evidence suggests that incarceration does not deter delinquents from committing additional crimes after they are released from confinement.

Violent crime is one of America's severest social problems, and it is particularly shocking when such crimes are committed by youths who seem to have no understanding of the serious harm they have caused.

Sometimes, especially in the wake of heinous and highly publicized crimes, the public becomes convinced that large numbers of our young people are predatory criminals who think nothing of killing or maiming innocent victims. At times like these citizens clamor for protection against young lawbreakers, and public officials respond with stiffer penalties for those offenders who are caught and convicted.

But this periodic cycle of public outrage followed by harsher punishment apparently has not reduced violent juvenile crime. Nor has it diminished the public's fear of such crimes. Therefore, it is now appropriate to reexamine our assumptions about youth violence to determine if our responses to the problem are based on the best available information. . . .

Rates of Violent Youth Crime

One common method of measuring crime is to look at arrest rates (although this method is imperfect because suspects who are arrested may not be representative of all those who commit crimes).

The latest *Uniform Crime Reports*—which are compiled by the Federal Bureau of Investigation based on statistics from local police departments—show that persons under 18 accounted for 17 percent of the 1985 arrests for the most serious violent offenses: murder, non-negligent manslaughter, rape, robbery, and aggravated assault. Among the more than 1.7 million arrests of juveniles in 1985, some 4 percent were for these serious violent crimes.[1]

The federal government also sponsors annual National Crime Surveys in which interviewers ask a representative sample of citizens about their experiences as victims of crime. In the survey for 1979, the latest from which we have data, victims attributed about 25 percent of the rapes, robberies, assaults, and larcenies to offenders under 18 years old.[2]

However, even though they commit fewer violent crimes than

adults, because juveniles are a relatively small part of the United States population, as a whole their *rate* of committing such crimes, is higher than the rate for adults, though it is lower than the rate for persons aged 18 to 20.[3]

While juvenile offenders account for a relatively small proportion of violent crimes, they are more apt to engage in property crimes. The 1985 *Uniform Crime Reports* show that juveniles accounted for 38 percent of the arrests for burglary and motor vehicle theft, 41 percent of the arrests for arson and 33 percent of the arrests for larceny.[4] Of the almost two million juvenile arrests in 1985, 4.1 percent involved serious violent crimes, 33 percent were serious property offenses, 34.7 percent were less serious offenses such as vandalism and assaults without weapons or injuries, and 28.1 percent involved noncriminal behavior such as truancy and running away from home.[5]. . .

Deterring Crimes by Young Offenders

The Columbus cohort study found that after being released from incarceration delinquents committed additional crimes at a faster rate than they had before.[6] Similarly, the Philadelphia cohort study concluded:

Not only do a greater number of those who receive punitive treatment (institutionalization, fine, or probation) continue to violate the law, but they also commit more serious crimes with greater rapidity than those who experience a less constraining contact with the judicial and correctional systems. Thus, we must conclude that the juvenile justice system, at its best, has no effect on the subsequent behavior of adolescent boys and, at its worst, has a deleterious effect on future behavior.[7]

One interpretation of these findings is that judges were correctly selecting for incarceration those youths most likely to commit further crimes after release.[8] Another interpretation is that the experience of incarceration itself encourages further delinquency because prisons and jails serve as "schools for crime." Biographical reports and fiction such as Clifford Shaw's *The Jack-Roller*, Claude Brown's *Manchild in the Promised Land,* and John Allen's *Assault with a Deadly Weapon,* do depict youths learning to become hardened criminals in such institutions.

Contrary to the findings above, a study of Chicago's UDIS (Unified Delinquency Intervention Services) program found that both incarceration and community-based programs reduced subsequent arrest rates. (Some scholars have attributed this finding to allegedly faulty research methods, but others defend the study.)[9]

Whatever the effects of incarceration on future criminality, there is abundant evidence that such institutions cause long-lasting psychological damage to many youths.[10]

Putting Violent Juveniles Behind Bars

Data from the Philadelphia cohort study indicate that putting twice as many juvenile offenders behind bars would result in a 1 to 4 percent reduction in theft, property damage, and sexual assaults.[11] Similarly, an Ohio study concluded that large increases in the incarceration of adult and juvenile offenders would have only minimal impact on the crime rate.[12]

In deciding how often to resort to incarceration, the benefits must be balanced against the high human and financial costs. In 1986, it cost from $20,000 to $51,000 per year to incarcerate each youth, which is far greater than the cost of community-based programs such as restitution and community service work.[13] Thus, a study prepared for Congress proposed that secure confinement ought to be treated as a "scarce resource" to be used only when all other possibilities have been exhausted.[14]

Getting Tough with Delinquents

Nationwide, a study estimates, at least half of the 450,000 juveniles held in detention each year could be released to supervised non-secure settings without endangering public safety if recognized national detention standards were enforced.[15]

The National Council on Crime and Delinquency completed a study in 1987 titled, "Adjudicated Youth in Delaware Who Need Secure Care." The study, based on the Ferris Training School, concluded that a great number of juveniles are incarcerated needlessly and that the same offenders would be better served in the community.

A Security Placement Instrument (SPI) was used for all youth committed to Ferris after May 1987. The findings were alarming. Delaware was clearly over-incarcerating its youth. Of the 133 youth in Ferris, 95 scored within the low range on the SPI and seemed to pose no threat to public safety. Special staffing and additional follow-up was needed for 32 youths, while only six youths were determined to need secure care.

Other states such as Massachusetts and Utah have been successful in minimizing training school populations by placing

THE NATIONAL COUNCIL ON CRIME AND DELINQUENCY

Reprinted with permission from the National Council on Crime and Delinquency.

offenders who qualify into community programs, without compromising public safety.[16] . . .

What Works with Violent Youths

An ideal way to deal with violent juveniles has yet to be developed. But, the current trend leans toward a combination of community-based programs and small secure facilities for the few violent juvenile offenders. As a result of research, a number of juvenile systems have successfully decreased their secure bed capacity. Community programs offer opportunities to learn social skills, education, and the chance for the offender to stay in the community while attempting rehabilitation.[17]

In 1980 the state of Utah closed its large training school, dropping the number of youth in secure beds from 350 to 60. Those released from the training school were placed in well-structured community programs.[18]

The Utah reform experience is regarded as an unqualified success. Utah's success is partially attributed to the implementation of a risk-screening system prior to closing the training school. Inmates were closely screened so that the high risk violent offenders were placed in the remaining secure beds, causing no threat to public safety.[19]

Placing youth back in their communities has proven to be highly productive. Studies show that youth who go through community-care have no higher rate of returning to crime than those youth who go to training schools.[20]

After examining a number of programs, some researchers believe there are certain ingredients crucial to a successful program. Among them are continuous case management, emphasis on reintegration and after-care services, opportunities for youth achievement and program decision-making, consistent and clear consequences for misconduct, educational and vocational programming, and individual and family counseling matched to youth needs.[21]

In order to respond most effectively to violent juvenile crime it is necessary to keep the problem in proper perspective. The facts outlined above show that most delinquency does not involve violence.

Nevertheless, it is clear that a relatively small proportion of juvenile lawbreakers do pose a serious threat to the safety of society. They need special attention from the juvenile justice system—intensive programs run by highly qualified staff. In some cases they need secure custody, but it should not be dehumanizing.

The juvenile justice system has limited resources. As long as it is swamped with hundreds of thousands of cases involving minor and even noncriminal offenses, it will not be able to deal adequately with the frightening but numerically small problem of violent juvenile delinquency.

Yet, broad demands to "get tough" with juvenile offenders often make it more difficult for the juvenile justice system to concentrate its limited resources on violent offenders. The "get tough" philosophy is so diffuse that it affects almost all youths who come into contact with the juvenile justice system. Harshness increases for both petty offenders and serious ones. The system soon finds its institutions crowded with young people who should not be in them.

Only when the juvenile justice system deals more efficiently with the large numbers of less serious offenders will it be able to respond more effectively to the serious dangers posed by repeat and violent offenders.

------

[1] Jamieson and Flanagan, 296.

[2] U.S. Bureau of Justice Statistics, 1981, 25.

[3] McDermott and Hindelang, 13.

[4] Webster, W.J., 174-175.

[5] Jamieson and Flanagan, 296.

[6] Hamparian et al., 101.

[7] Wolfgang, Figlio and Sellin, 252.

[8] Hamparian et al., 134.

[9] Murray and Cox; McCleary et al.

[10] Bartollas, Miller and Danitz; Newton.

[11] Clarke, 534.

[12] VanDine, Dinitz and Conrad, 112.

[13] Jamieson and Flanagan, 392.

[14] Abt Associates (1980), Volume 1, 130.

[15] Kihm, 28.

[16] DeMuro and Krisberg.

[17] Gendreau and Ross.

[18] Blackmore, Brown and Krisberg.

[19] Austin, Krisberg and Joe.

[20] Krisberg, discussion of Empey and Lubeck Silverlake Study, 18.

[21] Altschuler and Armstrong, 1984; Lindgren, 1984.

22   DEALING WITH URBAN VIOLENCE

JUVENILE OFFENDERS KNOW THEY WILL NOT BE PUNISHED

Patrick Buchanan

Patrick Buchanan is a conservative, syndicated columnist. His article appeared in the Conservative Chronicle.

Points to Consider:

1. Who is Richard Cohen? What was his response to the "wilding" attack that occurred in Central Park?

2. Does the author agree with Mr. Cohen's recommendation? Why or why not?

3. Historically, how did civilized nations put an end to savagery?

4. Why are we losing the war on crime?

Patrick Buchanan, "Gangs Know They Will Not Be Punished," *Conservative Chronicle,* May 10, 1989, p. 6. Reprinted by permission: Tribune Media Services.

Until America's war against crime is taken away from the talkers, and turned over to people who know how to wage it, the barbarians will prevail.

Coming from *Washington Post* columnist Richard Cohen, the line had impact. It was Cohen's response to what happened to that 28-year-old woman, jogging in Central Park. Ambushed by a wolf pack of a dozen teen-agers down from Harlem to go "wilding" in the park, she was chased down and beaten to the ground with a pipe, and had her face smashed with a brick; when she quit fighting, she was stripped, molested, gang-raped and left to die in a puddle.

A Recommended "War" Plan

"There are no excuses for this sort of thing," Cohen said, "Not poverty. Not hostility. Not boredom. Not even the depression and hopelessness which lead some ghetto kids to devalue their own lives and thus those of others as well." Good, I thought; finally, they're waking up.

Then, came Cohen's recommended "war" plan, which, being studied by the White House, "would entail the establishment of a task force of non-government experts. The task force would assemble the considerable numbers of studies already done on the underclass. It would also hold public hearings in various cities. . .to educate the public about the underclass. The preliminary focus would be on ways to revive inner-city institutions and attract bright, public-spirited people into the field, etc., etc. . . .the cost is bound to be steep. . . ."

We Don't Need Another Study

Excuse me, this is where I came in. The Great Society was going to deal with crime 25 years and a trillion dollars ago, remember.

Sorry, Richard, we don't have any more money for goo-goo experiments; and we don't need any more studies to tell us how to deal with savages for whom gang rape is "fun," as one of the wolf pack said from his cellblock.

How does a civilized, self-confident people deal with enemies who gang-rape their women? Armies stand them up against a wall, and shoot them; or we hang them, as we did the Japanese and Nazi war criminals. If, while Mr. Cohen's experts were perusing position papers on the underclass, the eldest of that wolf pack were tried, convicted and hanged in Central Park, by

142

WILD CREATURES

The events in Central Park can be viewed through at least four prisms: race, class, gender, and generation. But so far, generation has been invoked principally in astonishment at the tender age of the accused—two are 14, three 15—as if nobody that young could be so ferocious.

But adolescents—black or white, poor or privileged—tend to be wild creatures, given the surges of feeling they cannot comprehend, to bouts of violence, to cruelty. That lesson is underlined by the arrest last month of five white teenagers in the affluent New Jersey suburb of Glen Ridge for the sexual assault of a mentally handicapped girl. According to the FBI, about 46 percent of all violent crimes reported in America during 1987 were committed by youths between ages 10 and 24.

J. Anthony Lukas, "Boyhood Brings With It a Culture of Easy Brutality," Star Tribune, *June 4, 1989*

June 1; and the 13- and 14-year olds were stripped, horsewhipped and sent to prison, the park might soon be safe again for women.

Juveniles Are Unafraid

Historically, civilized nations have put an end to savagery by a traditional means. With their conquering armies, they put the fear of death into the barbarians; then, with religious conversions, either coerced or voluntary, they instilled the fear of God. Thus, did self-confident nations "civilize" the barbarians.

Today, we cannot instill in the children of the inner cities a fear of God, a hatred of sin, and a love of their fellow man, because the ACLU forbids it; and we cannot instill in them the fear of death, because Governor Mario Cuomo will not permit it.

The wolf pack entered Central Park unafraid, for the best of reasons; it had nothing to fear. If caught by the police, they would be unharmed; if convicted, their lives were secure. No wonder they were joking in their jail cells; they have the personal guarantee of the governor of New York that even if that brutalized woman dies of her fractured skull, they are safe from the electric chair.

143

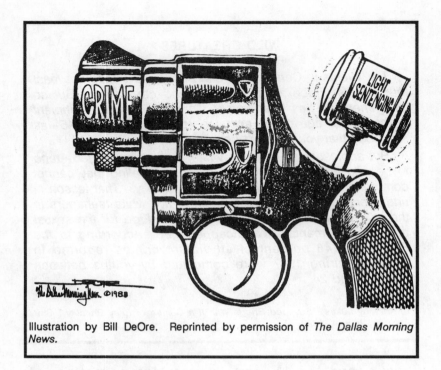

Illustration by Bill DeOre. Reprinted by permission of *The Dallas Morning News*.

Losing the War on Crime

Calling the atrocity the "ultimate shriek of alarm," Governor Cuomo cautioned us against letting popular rage get out of control: "They'll say you don't need a trial, you don't need a search warrant, you don't need Miranda." Leave it to Mario, at a time like this, to be worried about a Warren court decision which says that New York police must be sure to warn the animals not to blurt out something that might incriminate them for what they just did.

Mr. Cohen sees a need to "attract bright, public-spirited citizens." But, if there is a war on, we need, first, to arm and equip our troops, the cops, and turn them loose on the enemy with the kind of backing we gave our troops in World War II. We won that war, remember, Richard. But, we can't do that, because we are too busy tying the cops' hands, deploring "police brutality," denouncing "racist attitudes," setting up review boards to hear civilian gripes, making sure members of the wolf pack are treated with courtesy, and, of course, read their Miranda rights.

We are losing the war on crime, because our troops are demoralized, and the enemy is unafraid; and we will not win the war on crime until the fear that was pounding in that poor girl's heart, as the pack was running her down, is transferred to the hearts of the savages who assaulted her.

Barbarians Will Prevail

It wasn't always thus. Some of us grew up on films about tough lawmen coming to town to string up horse thieves, and shoot down bank robbers, and about bounty hunters who brought back killers, dead or alive. The films were all about: *How the West Was Won.*

Well, the West is being lost today because our great cities and their public parks, centers of our civilization, are being captured by barbarians, and because we lack the moral clear-sightedness to see our enemies for who they are, and the moral authority to treat them as what they are.

Paralyzed with guilt, equating evil with illness, worshipping "process," and "procedure," our Lords Temporal have lost sight of the first purpose of law: *Salus populi,* the safety of the people. Until America's war against crime is taken away from the talkers, and turned over to people who know how to wage it, the barbarians will prevail, and, we probably ought to get our women out of the parks.

23 DEALING WITH URBAN VIOLENCE

CUT MILITARY SPENDING AND GIVE MORE AID TO CITIES

Bulletin of Municipal Foreign Policy

The Bulletin of Municipal Foreign Policy is a quarterly publication of the Local Elected Officials Project of the Center for Innovative Diplomacy.

Points to Consider:

1. What did the U.S. Conference of Mayors' study reveal?

2. How do national leaders define national security? What does national security mean to most Americans and many of America's mayors?

3. Describe the study produced by Employment Research Associates (ERA).

4. How does ERA's study differ from other reports?

"Pentagon Cut Would Help Cities, Mayors' Study Concludes," *Bulletin of Municipal Foreign Policy,* Winter 1988-89, pp.42-43.

National security means more than weapons. It means strong families and strong neighborhoods. Measured in these terms, our national security has been breached.

A U.S. Conference of Mayors' study released in October found that a $30 billion transfer from military to domestic programs—a 10 percent cut in the Pentagon's current budget—would improve the quality of life in the nation's cities and towns by boosting the nation's Gross National Product (GNP) and creating nearly 200,000 new jobs.

The Conference President, Mayor Arthur Holland of Trenton, New Jersey, applauded the 50-page report, entitled "A Shift in Military Spending to America's Cities."

"The results are. . . .clear," Holland said. "Investing in the cities is really investing in America. What works for the cities works for the nation."

"National Security"

Irvine, California, Mayor Larry Agran, who authored the Conference's National Priorities Resolution originally calling for the study, said the report added weight to his charge that both presidential candidates had ignored "real national security."

"The candidates speak often of their commitment to strong national security. But to most Americans—including many of America's mayors," Agran said, "the candidates speak a foreign language. They talk of national security only in the narrowest terms. They speak of Trident submarines, MX missiles, and Star Wars. In short, they equate massive, even wasteful, military spending with national security.

"Mayors worry about national security, too," Agran said. "But to us, national security means more than weapons. It means strong families and strong neighborhoods in economically vibrant communities. It means good-paying jobs in modern industries that are competitive in the global marketplace. It means health care and education, child care, and transportation worthy of our citizens. It means decent, affordable housing for every American.

"Measured in these terms, our national security has been breached. Our cities are under siege."

Chicago Mayor Eugene Sawyer agreed, saying increases in military spending have come at the expense of America's cities.

HOW A PENTAGON CUT WOULD HELP CHICAGO

"Both Chicago's unemployment rate, and the share of its households living below the poverty level, are well above the national average. The city's aging transportation and housing infrastructure is in need of extensive renovation. . . "

"The change envisioned in this study would more than double existing federal support to Chicago and Cook County in the areas of housing and community development, education and job training, mass transit, and health and social services."

Overall, Chicago would show "a substantial gain in its Gross Regional Product and a net annual gain of 20,020 jobs."

"Pentagon Cut Would Help Cities, Mayors' Study Concludes," Bulletin of Municipal Foreign Policy, *Winter 1988-89, p. 43*

"The lack of federal funding in recent years has directly and indirectly caused many of the social ills we are experiencing in our urban areas today—housing, economic development, education, job training, mass transit, health and social services cutbacks. . . .cities teeming with drug-related crime and our jail cells overflowing."

Employment Research Association

The study was produced by Employment Research Associates (ERA) of Lansing, Michigan, and documents the likely impact of a $30 billion annual transfer—$150 billion over five years (1986-1990)—from military spending to what Agran called "programs of proven effectiveness in our cities and towns."

Marion Anderson, ERA's Executive Director, said "A Shift in Military Spending" is very different from previous studies of the military impact on the domestic economy.

"Other reports have said, 'It would be very nice if you could hire new teachers,'" Anderson said. "Well, we're not just showing that you can hire new teachers if you cut military spending. We're showing the impact of those new teachers spending money in the economies of four cities and in the national economy."

Illustration by David Seavey. Copyright 1983, *USA Today*. Reprinted with permission.

Urban Economies

The study analyzed how a national shift in budget priorities would affect the economies of Trenton, New Jersey; Chicago, Illinois; Irvine, California; and Austin, Texas. These cities were deemed to be representative of the country: Trenton because it represents the nation's older established Northeastern cities; Chicago because it represents the Midwestern industrial heartland; high-tech Irvine, California, which is the heart of a military-dependent region; and Austin, Texas, an economically diverse Southwestern city.

"To our knowledge, nothing like this has ever been done," Anderson said of the study. "It has a specificity based on real data and based on real cities, not just some generic city."

In focusing on urban economies, however, the Conference

study has not missed the forest for the trees. At the end of five years, the study concludes, the transfer of $30 billion to domestic priorities could provide each year the construction or renovation of nearly one million homes, the hiring of 387,000 new teachers, aides and support staff, the enhancement of rapid transit systems, new public health projects, and a wide array of child care, senior service and job-training programs.

MORE MONEY FOR URBAN PROBLEMS WON'T HELP

Warren T. Brookes

Warren T. Brookes is a syndicated columnist. His article appeared in the Conservative Chronicle.

Points to Consider:

1. How does Washington, D.C.'s spending compare to other big cities and other state and local averages?

2. Why are D.C. shops unable to attract retail sales help?

3. Has social spending helped Washington, D.C.? Please explain your answer.

Warren T. Brookes, "D.C. Is the Liberals' National Embarrassment," *Conservative Chronicle,* January 25, 1989, p. 22. © 1989 - Permission of Creators Syndicate, Inc.

Washington is living proof that throwing really big money at city problems only makes those problems worse, unless you know what makes people and cities tick.

Just as 50,000 inauguration guests and players start arriving, Washington, D.C., Mayor Marion Barry has become the target of vicious venom from liberals, and not just because of his repeated and embarrassing associations with folks accused of drug dealing.

A Dismal Swamp

His bloated, mismanaged, and corrupt city government and its highest-in-the-nation spending is the paradigm for the monumental failures of American liberal social policies.

If the sheer amount of social spending were the key to urban harmony and well-being, Washington would be the Eden of western democracy. Instead, it is one of its most dismal swamps.

Social Spending Hasn't Helped

For example, Washington now spends nearly $5,800 a year per student on public education, nearly 50 percent above the national average. It pays its teachers the second highest level in the nation, close to a $35,000 a year average. Yet, its drop out rate (48 percent) is the worst in the nation and its SAT scores are third from the bottom.

The city spends 2.7 times the national per capita rate on welfare and food stamps. Yet, poverty in Washington is 50 percent higher than the national average. Among children, it is almost 70 percent above the national average, and its soup kitchens are routinely full.

It spends over five times as much per capita on housing and community development as the average of all major cities, and is one of only nine U.S. cities with long-term rent control. Yet, it has one of the three worst levels of homelessness in the nation.

A Spending Disgrace

It spends 2.1 times the state and local average on health and hospital care. Yet, it has the highest infant mortality rate in the nation. Among blacks, its infant mortality is 30 percent higher than in the rural south. Its overall death rate is 54 percent above the nation, the worst.

152

GANGS REFLECT SOCIETY'S VALUES

Look at the comments attributed to gang members. What are the salient concerns? First, a lust after money as the primary goal. Second, an acceptance of violence as a means of obtaining money or other goods. Third, a juvenile fixation with power and power structures. This is hardly new stuff.

"Money. That's the only thing. Makes me want to live."

Money. Wealth. Prestige. Accumulation of possessions. Consumption as an end in itself. Forget about genuine human need. Haven't they learned their lessons well? In school or not, I'd still score them an "A" in Assimilation of the Dominant Values of Society.

Tom Boswell, *"Gangs Just Living Out Society's Values,"* The Milwaukee Journal, *February 1, 1984*

One reason for this astonishing death rate is Washington's worst-in-the nation homicide rate. In 1988 there were 371 murders in D.C., more than one a day, and most of them drug-related. This is a murder rate of 61 per 100,000 population, seven times the national average of 8.5, making it the U.S. murder capital as well.

Yet, Washington spends over twice as much on police and fire protection as the average for all large cities: Nearly $400 per capita on these services compared with $239 for New York, $180 for Los Angeles, $228 for Detroit, $196 for Philadelphia.

Washington's streets are among the worst maintained in the nation. A three-inch snowfall can tie the city up for days. Yet Washington spends 43 percent more than all cities spend on road and street maintenance, and double or triple what is being spent in cities like New York, Chicago, Philadelphia, even snow-bound Boston, and 30 percent more than wintry Minneapolis.

The Employment Situation

Marion Barry's disgusting make-work, crony-laden government employs an astonishing 40,000 people. That's 633 city workers for every 10,000 people. The national average for big cities is 224. Even if you accept that D.C. is more like a city-state than city alone, its payroll level is 43 percent above the average for all state and local governments combined.

Despite this appalling level of direct D.C. government employment, and the nation's most labor-short marketplace (with government unemployment averaging less than 2 percent) the city's black unemployment rate remains stuck at about 7 percent.

Yet, the most common sign in D.C. shops, stores, and businesses these days is "help wanted." Retail sales clerk jobs paying $6-$7 per hour and fringe benefits are going begging. In Alexandria, Virginia, a subway ride from the city, school custodial and cafeteria jobs at over $6 per hour have been empty for months and employees are being paid $100 savings bonds as a bonus to recruit workers. The minimum wage is irrelevant in the tightest labor market in the United States.

As a Virginia employment commissioner told the *Washington Post,* "We're in a full employment area. There just aren't any people to attract, even if they paid $10 an hour."

To put it bluntly, there is not the slightest excuse for anyone in Washington being either homeless or hungry if they are able-bodied. But Washington's underclass grows worse off.

A Bureaucratic Machine

This, not his drug skirmishes, is why Marion Barry has become the target of liberal pundits like Mary McGrory who called him "a big city boss in the style of Richard Daley of Chicago."

That's not fair to Daley, who ran the city of Chicago with among the lowest operating expenses of any city in the nation — less than half the comparable costs of Barry's Washington bureaucratic machine.

No, it isn't only Barry's corruption (the *Washington Monthly* brilliantly documents it as "The Worst City Government in America"). It's that Washington is living proof that throwing really big money at city problems only makes those problems worse, unless you know what makes people and cities tick.

Barry has proved that most liberals don't even have a clue.

WHAT IS EDITORIAL BIAS?

This activity may be used as an individualized study guide for students in libraries and resource centers or as a discussion catalyst in small group and classroom discussions.

The capacity to recognize an author's point of view is an essential reading skill. The skill to read with insight and understanding involves the ability to detect different kinds of opinions or bias. Sex bias, race bias, ethnocentric bias, political bias, and religious bias are five basic kinds of opinions expressed in editorials and all literature that attempts to persuade. They are briefly defined below.

Five Kinds of Editorial Opinions or Bias

SEX BIAS—The expression of dislike for and/or feeling of superiority over the opposite sex or a particular sexual minority

RACE BIAS—The expression of dislike for and/or feeling of superiority over a racial group

ETHNOCENTRIC BIAS—The expression of a belief that one's own group, race, religion, culture, or nation is superior. Ethnocentric persons judge others by their own standards and values

POLITICAL BIAS—The expression of political opinions and attitudes about domestic or foreign affairs

RELIGIOUS BIAS—The expression of a religious belief or attitude

---

Guidelines

1. From the readings in Chapter Four, locate five sentences that provide examples of editorial opinion or bias.

2. Write down each of the above sentences and determine what kind of bias each sentence represents. Is it *sex bias, race bias, ethnocentric bias, political bias, or religious bias?*

3. Make up one sentence statements that would be an example of each of the following: *sex bias, race bias, ethnocentric bias, political bias, and religious bias.*

4. See if you can locate five sentences that are factual statements from the readings in Chapter Four.

BIBLIOGRAPHY I

An Overview on Inner-City Violence

Bader, Eleanor J. "Texas Gang Rape Gets Little Media." *Guardian*, 27 April 1988, p. 2.

Baker, J. N. "Crack Wars in D.C." *Newsweek,* 22 February 1988, p. 24.

Bing, L. "Reflections of a Gangbanger." *Harper's*, August 1988, pp. 26+.

Bloom, Marie. "Survival and Nonviolence." *The Nonviolent Activist,* April/May 1988, p. 9-12.

Booker, Chris. "The Black 'Underclass.'" *Guardian,* 28 December 1988, p. 10-11.

Booker, Chris. "Urban League: Wipe Out Racism by Year 2000." *Guardian,* 22 February 1989, p. 7.

Brownfeld, Allan C. "How Our Criminal Justice System Serves Convicts." *Human Events*, 22 April 1989, p. 12-15.

Burgos, J. "Husband Tosses Wife 18 Stories in Heated Dispute." *Jet,* 26 October 1987, *pp. 32.*

Carlson, Allan. "How Uncle Sam Got in the Family's Way. *Wall Street Journal,* 20 April 1988.

Carlson, M. B. "Five Friends in a Car." *Time*, 11 July 1988, p. 20.

Cone, James. "Confronting Violence and Vengeance." *International Christian Digest,* April 1987, p. 33-35.

Cook, J. "The Worms in the Big Apple." *Forbes*, 21 September 1987, p. 102-6.

"Crime: Fighting Public Enemy No. 1." *Scholastic Update,* 4 December 1987, p. 2-20.

"Crime in the Cities: The Drug Connection" *Newsweek,* 1 February 1988, p. 47.

Czerny, Clara. "Death to Desire." *New Internationalist*, September 1988, p. 11-12.

Daly, M. "The Fat Man: The Life and High Times of Irwin Schiff." *New York,* 19 October 1987, p. 46-61.

"The Drug Gangs." *Newsweek*, 28 March 1988, pp. 20-25.

"Ethnic Gangs and Organized Crime." *U.S. News and World Report,* 18 January 1988, pp. 29-31.

Galef, D. "Incident in the Park." *New York Times Magazine,* 8 February 1987, p. 56.

Gonzalez, D. L. "Drug Gangs: The Big Sweep." *Newsweek*, 24 October 1988, p. 26.

Hackett, G. and Lerner, M. A. "L.A. Law: Gangs and Crack." *Newsweek,* 27 April 1987, pp. 35-36.

Harvey, Paul. "Street Gangs Have Long Tentacles." *Conservative Chronicle,* 29 April 1987, p. 10.

Hersch, P. "Coming of Age on the City Streets." *Psychology Today,* January 1988, pp. 28-32.

Hillhouse, R. "Crime in America: The Shocking Truth." *McCalls,* March 1987, p. 30.

"House of Horrors." *Time*, 6 April 1987, p. 34.

Hull, J. D. "Life and Death with the Gangs." *Time*, 24 August 1987, p. 41.

Johnson, T. E. "Urban Murders: On the Rise." *Newsweek,* 9 February 1987, p. 30.

Jones, Ann. "One Woman Who Chose to Say No." *The Nation,* 17 April 1982, p. 456-459.

Kasindorf, J. "Working Girl." *New York,* 18 April 1988, pp. 56-7.

Kelly, Ronald D. "Protect Your Children from Sexual Abuse." *The Plain Truth,* September 1988, p. 10-11.

Kendall, George A. "Sex, Violence, and Foreign Policy: A Response to Dale Vree." *The Wanderer,* 17 March 1988.

"L. A. Gangs Reported Moving into Other Cities." *Minneapolis Star-Tribune,* 14 July 1988.

Lamar, J. V. "A Bloody West Coast Story." *Time*, 18 April 1988, p. 32.

"Machine Gunman, High on Crack, Pumps 26 Fatal Bullets into Boy, 3." *Jet,* 7 December 1987, p. 36.

McCarthy, A. "No Safe Place." *Commonweal,* 10 February 1989, p. 72.

Morganthau, T. "Losing the War?" *Newsweek,* 14 March 1988, pp. 16-18.

Murray, C. A. "Crime in America." *National Review,* 10 June 1988, pp. 34-38.

Newlund, Sam. "Obsessed with Sex." *Minneapolis Star and Tribune*, 6 December 1988.

Ode, Kim. "Defining Rape Can Be Difficult in Some Cases." *Minneapolis Star and Tribune,* 16 January 1986, p. 1C.

Pfaff, William. "Racism and America's Moral Void." *Minneapolis Star Tribune*, 7 May 1988.

"Police: Jacqueline Wilson Innocent Victim of Slaying." *Jet,* 19 September 1988, p. 18.

Rheinhold, R. "In the Middle of LA's Gang Warfare." *The New York Times Magazine,* 22 May 1988, pp. 30-33.

Rosenbaum, R. "Crack Murder: A Detective Story." *New York Times Magazine,* 15 February 1987, pp. 24-30.

Rosenbaum, R. "Breaking the Crack Murders." *New York Times Magazine,* 13 November 1987, pp. 44-6.

Rowan, R. "The Mafia's Bite of the Big Apple." *Fortune,* 6 June 1988, pp. 128-30.

"Savage Ride." *Time,* 7 March 1988, p. 24.

"Shoot him! Shoot him!" *Time,* 8 February 1988, p. 33.

Schuchman, Miriam. "Victims of Rape: Where Can They Turn?" *The Progressive,* July 1981, p. 27-30.

"Slaughter in the Streets." *Time,* 5 December 1988, p. 32.

Staples, B. "A Commercial Overture." *New York Times Magazine*, 20 September 1987, p. 106.

Steacy, A. "Gunfire in Traffic." *Macleans,* 17 August 1987, pp. 21-22.

Stephens, G. "Crime and Punishment: Forces Shaping the Future." *Futurist,* January/February 1987, pp. 18-26.

"Street Sweepers." *U.S. News and World Report,* 25 April 1988, p. 14.

Traub, J. "The Lords of Hell's Kitchen." *New York Times Magazine,* 5 April 1987, p. 38.

Will, George F. "Military Patrols Won't Solve Problems in Nation's Capital." *Minneapolis Star-Tribune*, 9 April 1989.

Will, George F. "Problems of the Rich Inherited by the Poor." *Conservative Chronicle,* 18 January 1989, p. 29.

Will, G. F. "A 'West Coast Story'." *Newsweek,* 28 March 1988, p. 76.

Will, George F. "Why Can We See No Evil Where Evil Is Real?" *St. Paul Pioneer Press*, 30 April 1989.

BIBLIOGRAPHY II (ANNOTATED)

Juvenile Delinquency in the United States

Acock, Alan C. Clair, Jeffrey M. *The Influence of the Family: A Review and Annotated Bibliography of Socialization, Ethnicity, and Delinquency, 1975-1986.* New York, Garland, 1986. 315 p. (Garland reference library of social science, v. 353; Garland library of sociology, v. 9) Z7164.Y8A26 1986 HQ796

Includes bibliographies and index.

Bartollas, Clemens. *Juvenile Delinquency.* New York, Wilay, 1985. 633p. HV9104.B345 1985

Partial contents. — The measurement of official delinquency. — The causes of delinquency. — Environmental influences on delinquency in America. — The female and male delinquent. — Juvenile corrections. — Primary and secondary prevention, treatment, and the summary.

Families, Schools, and Delinquency Prevention. James Q. Wilson and Glenn C. Loury, editors. New York, Springer-Verlag, 1987. 340 p. (From Children to Citizens, v. 3) HV741.F35 1987

Focuses on family social work and the role of the schools in preventing juvenile delinquency.

Gibbons, Don C. *Delinquent Behavior*, by Don C. Gibbons and Marvin D. Krohn. 4th ed. Englewood Cliffs, N.J., Prentice-Hall, 1986. 285 p. HV9104.G53 1986

Partial contents. — The study of delinquency. — Delinquency causation: — basic considerations. — Social status, opportunity, and delinquency. — Cultural values, social learning, and delinquency. — Biological and psychological perspectives on delinquency. — Alternatives to incarceration.

— — — — —. "Juvenile Delinquency: Can Social Science Find a Cure?" *Crime and Delinquency*, v. 32, Apr. 1986: 186-204. LRS86-3637

Explains a trend among criminologists toward pessimism regarding the causes of or treatment for delinquency. Recommends traditional prevention efforts be discontinued in favor of efforts for diversion of status and minor offenders.

Kids, Drugs, and Crime, by Cheryl Carpenter and others. Lexington, Mass., Lexington Books, 1988. 244 p. HV5824.Y68K52 1988

Partial contents. — Adolescents' perspectives on the relationship between drugs/alcohol and crime. — Theft and the consumeristic mentality. — Case studies of youths at risk in early adolescence. — The deterrent effect of adult versus juvenile jurisdiction.

Kratcosky, Peter C. Kratcoski, Lucille Dunn. *Juvenile Delinquency.* Englewood Cliffs, N.J., Prentice-Hall, 1986. 389 p. HV9104.K7 1986

Explores "the problems of youthful deviance and unlawful behavior in the United States, and the methods used to inhibit, detect, punish, deter, or reduce the recurrence of such activity."

Lamar, Jacob V. "Kids Who Sell Crack." *Time*, v. 131, May 9, 1988: 20-24, 27, 30, 33. LRS88-2975

"The drug trade has become the nation's newest — and most frightening — job program. . . .Teenagers have come to dominate all aspects of the crack business."

Lotz, Roy. Poole, Eric D. Regoli, Robert M. *Juvenile Delinquency and Juvenile Justice.* New York, Random House, 1985. 408 p. HV9104.L67 1985

Partial contents. — Public perceptions of crime and delinquency. — Family and delinquency. — Schools and delinquency. — Adolescence, peers, and delinquency. — The contemporary juvenile court. — Critical issues in juvenile justice.

Patterson, Gerald R. Dishion, Thomas J. "Contributions of Families and Peers to Delinquency." *Criminology,* v. 23, Feb. 1985: 63-79. LRS85-10013

"A model is presented that explains the contribution of parents and peers to adolescent delinquent behavior. . . .Poor parent monitoring, deviant peers, and low levels of academic skills are hypothesized to contribute directly to an adolescent's engagement in delinquent behavior."

Pelham, Ann. "Teen Curfews Are Popular in Cities Again." *Governing,* v. 1, Apr. 1988: 60-62. LRS88-1818

"Sporadically, U.S. communities frustrated by unruly teen-agers have turned to curfews. No national tally of curfew ordinances is kept, and even those laws on the books are often not enforced."

Reinhold, Robert. "In the Middle of L.A.'s Gang Warfare." *New York Times Magazine,* May 22, 1988: 30, 33, 66-67, 70, 74. LRS88-4062

Examines the growing street gang problem in Los Angeles. Author discusses the crime resulting from these gangs, and the various police and community agency efforts to ease the tension.

Siegel, Larry J. Senna, Joseph J. *Juvenile Delinquency.* 3rd ed. St. Paul, West Pub. Co., 1988. 616 p. HV9104.S53 1988

Partial contents.— The nature of delinquency.— Focus on law-status offense law.— Official data sources.— Beyond cocaine: crack, basuco, and freebase.— Start.— Labeling and social conflict theory.— Female delinquents.— The family's influence on delinquency.— Child abuse and neglect.— Juvenile gangs and groups.— Schools and delinquency.— Juvenile courts and the law.— Police work with juveniles.— Pretrial procedures.— The juvenile trial and disposition.— Juvenile corrections.— Institutionalization and aftercare.

Snyder, Howard N. Finnegan, Terrence A. *Delinquency in the United States, 1983.* Washington, U.S. National Institute of Juvenile Justice and Delinquency Prevention, 1987. 45 p. LRS87-5613

Describes the volume and characteristics of delinquency and status offense cases disposed in 1983 by courts with juvenile jurisdiction, . . .an estimated 1,247,000 delinquency and status offense cases. This represents a four percent decline over the 1982 level. . . .The decline in the number of status offense cases reflects a general policy over this time period of transferring the primary responsibility for status offenders (e.g., runaways, truants, and ungovernables) from the juvenile courts to child welfare agencies.

Trojanowicz, Robert C. Morash, Merry. *Juvenile Delinquency: Concepts and Control.* Englewood Cliffs, N.J., Prentice-Hall, 1987. 484 p. HV9104.T76 1987

Partial contents. — Issues in understanding juvenile delinquency. — Theories of delinquency causation. — The family and juvenile delinquency. — Handling the juvenile delinquent within the juvenile justice system. — Delinquency prevention programs. — Juveniles with multiple problems.

Juvenile Courts and Corrections

Belknap, Joanne. Morash, Merry. Trojanowicz, Robert. "Implementing a Community Policing Model for Work with Juveniles: An Exploratory Study." *Criminal Justice and Behavior,* v. 14, June 1987: 211-245. LRS87-5778

"Theories of role identity were used to determine officers' ideal, actual, and behavioral identities in interactions with teenagers, complainants, and supervisors when dealing with a case of 'rowdy teens.' A purposive sample was drawn representing foot and motor patrol, as well as race (black and white) and gender. The findings support the implementation of the community police model as was intended by the staff, and suggests the validity of the foot patrol concept."

"Juvenile Justice: Special Issue." *Law & Policy* , v. 8, Oct. 1986: whole issue (389-528 p.) LRS86-13413

Partial contents. — The Juvenile Justice and Delinquency Prevention Act: Federal leadership in State reform, by Gordon A. Raley and John E. Dean. — Reforming justice by geography: organizational responses to the problem of juvenile crime, by Susan Guarino Ghezzi and Lee Kimbalol. — The politics of policy: deinstitutionalization in Massachusetts 1970-1985, by Bruce Bullington and others.

Koller, Benedict J. Tanner, Michael D. "Changing Attitudes Toward Juvenile Crime." *State Factor,* v. 13, May 1987: whole issue (12 p.) LRS87-4640

Partial contents. — The problem: skyrocketing juvenile crime. — A short history of the juvenile justice system. — The legislative response. — Towards a new juvenile justice system.

"Race and Juvenile Justice." *Crime and Delinquency,* v. 33, Apr. 1987: 173-286.

Contents. — The incarceration of minority youth (LRS87-5497). — Juvenile offenders: prevalence, offender incidence and arrest rates by race (LRS87-3810). — Blind justice? The impact of race on the juvenile justice process (LRS87-5586). — Racial determinants of the judicial transfer decision: prosecuting violent youth in criminal court (LRS87-3811).

WATERLOO HIGH SCHOOL LIBRARY
1464 INDUSTRY RD.
ATWATER, OHIO 44201

DATE DUE

DEC 8			
DEC 15			

DEMCO 38-297

Inner city violence   13701
McCuen, Gary   303.6 McC